Qualitative Research and the
Modern Library

CHANDOS
INFORMATION PROFESSIONAL SERIES

Series Editor: Ruth Rikowski
(email: Rikowskigr@aol.com)

Chandos' new series of books is aimed at the busy information professional. They have been specially commissioned to provide the reader with an authoritative view of current thinking. They are designed to provide easy-to-read and (most importantly) practical coverage of topics that are of interest to librarians and other information professionals. If you would like a full listing of current and forthcoming titles, please visit our web site www.chandospublishing.com or email info@chandospublishing.com or telephone +44 (0) 1223 499140.

New authors: we are always pleased to receive ideas for new titles; if you would like to write a book for Chandos, please contact Dr Glyn Jones on e-mail gjones@chandospublishing .com or telephone number +44 (0) 1993 848726.

Bulk orders: some organisations buy a number of copies of our books. If you are interested in doing this, we would be pleased to discuss a discount. Please contact on email info@chandospublishing.com or telephone +44 (0) 1223 499140.

Qualitative Research and the Modern Library

VALEDA DENT GOODMAN

CP

CHANDOS
PUBLISHING

Oxford Cambridge New Delhi

Chandos Publishing
Hexagon House
Avenue 4
Station Lane
Witney
Oxford OX28 4BN
UK
Tel: +44 (0) 1993 848726
Email: info@chandospublishing.com
www.chandospublishing.com

Chandos Publishing is an imprint of Woodhead Publishing Limited

Woodhead Publishing Limited
80 High Street
Sawston
Cambridge CB22 3HJ
UK
Tel: +44 (0) 1223 499140
Fax: +44 (0) 1223 832819
www.woodheadpublishing.com

First published in 2011

ISBN:
978 1 84334 644 9

British Library Cataloguing-in-Publication Data.
A catalogue record for this book is available from the British Library.

Typeset by RefineCatch Limited, Bungay, Suffolk
Printed in the UK and USA.

This book is dedicated to my husband Geoff, who stuck with me through the writing of this book—definitely not an easy task! His laughter, thirst for knowledge, and curiosity are always the best part of my day.

To my nephews Trent Jr., Justin, and Howard IV: you have filled my life with such wonder and happiness.

And to my very best friend, Chantal, who let me turn her home into a writer's retreat in order to get this book finished. She teaches me something new about kindness and patience every day.

Contents

List of figures and tables   xi
Acknowledgments   xiii
Author biography   xv

Introduction   1

1   A brief overview of qualitative research   7

    A description of qualitative research   8
    Gathering the data   10
    A little bit about grounded theory   20
    A little bit about analyzing the data   22
    Challenges to working with qualitative data   24
    References   26

2   Examples of qualitative research in non-library
    settings   33

    Becoming a student: research in an academic
    environment   33
    A.C. Nielsen Company as an example of rich
    media research   35
    Qualitative research in nursing   38
    Qualitative research in medicine and mental
    health disciplines   40
    References   41

Contents

3 Ethnographic research practices in library settings   **45**

Key concepts of ethnographic research   45

Historical application within libraries and
information settings   50

Examples of recent ethnographic research in
library environments   56

Balancing quantitative and qualitative approaches
to library research   64

Implications and challenges   66

References   68

**4 Eyes wide open: using trends, professional
literature, and users to create a research canvas
in libraries**   **75**

Generational differences and the digital
landscape   79

The state of the research and academic library   85

Understanding the role of technology through
research   90

The matrix: a tool for the beginning   96

References   98

**5 Inside the mind of the user: qualitative
approaches to understanding user experience in
library settings**   **107**

The self and user experience   109

Design, broken-ness, and the library user
experience   111

Useit.com on UX research   115

Flow as an element of the user experience   117

References   120

6   Narrowing the field: using qualitative approaches
    to explore specific areas of interest   125

    The library is still scary—a new look at reference
    by way of an old concept   125

    Still with us: the library website (The Rutgers Study)   130

    Disruption and the information seeker   134

    References   139

7   What about us? Using qualitative methods to
    explore the library as workplace   147

    References   151

8   A place in the world: qualitative research as a
    way to study global libraries   157

    Why use a qualitative approach?   158

    The role of the rural village library   161

    Elements of the project's methods   163

    What the content analysis revealed   165

    References   172

9   Learning more about qualitative research   177

    References   182

10 Qualitative research as a way to explore change
    in the modern world   185

Index   187

List of figures and tables

Figure

4.1   Information Resource Data Collection   97

Tables

4.1   Matrix for Use during the Brainstorming
      Phase   98
8.1   Summary of Repeating Ideas, Themes and
      Theoretical Constructs   166

Acknowledgments

This is my second time working with Chandos Publishing, and once again I am grateful for the support provided by Glyn Jones throughout the writing of this book. I am also thankful for the help provided by Jonathan Davis, also from Chandos, who continually reached out to me to make sure all was well. My cousin, Anne Berry, is responsible for the beautiful cover of this book. My husband, Geoff, spent hours talking with me about qualitative research—conversations which provided a lot of motivation for me. Finally, I'd like to thank Dr. Heting Chu, whose class on qualitative research, which I took in the middle of writing this book, informed my thinking on the topic to even greater levels.

Author biography

Valeda Dent Goodman is a second-generation librarian who is currently Dean and Chief Operating Officer for the libraries at Long Island University in New York. She previously served as the Associate University Librarian for Research and Instructional Services at Rutgers University in New Brunswick, New Jersey; as Head of the reference division at the Hunter College Library in New York; and as project director for the MALIBU digital library project in London, United Kingdom. Valeda holds a Master's degree in Social Work and a Master's degree in Information Science, both from the University of Michigan. She is the author of numerous articles and has been published in a variety of academic journals. Valeda has a variety of research interests, including rural village libraries, user experience, instructional design, and experience design, and she has presented her research at both national and international venues. Her first book was published in May 2009, and she is currently working on her next manuscript on the impact of rural village libraries in Africa. Valeda lives in Westchester, New York, with her husband, Geoff, a child psychologist, and is currently pursuing her doctorate degree at the Palmer School of Information Science at Long Island University, New York.

Introduction

What do you think of when you hear the word "research"? When I first learned this as a vocabulary word in grade school, I remember thinking that it meant looking for something once, then looking for it again—doing a "re"-search. In actuality, that description is not too far off the mark. Research is the practice of discovery, and there are many different roads that can be taken to find what you are looking for.

Research means different things to different people. If you are a student, you might think of a research paper that you had to write. A pharmaceutical historian might think of the brutal Tuskegee drug research trials. My husband, who is a child psychologist, thinks about one of his favorite research studies, the "strange situation" studies conducted by Mary Ainsworth in the 1960s to learn more about children and their attachment to their caregivers. Regardless of the topic, research is a way to help reveal hidden information, answers, and clues about the world around us. It has become such a part of modern-day society that many of us just assume that most of what we eat, watch, are treated for, and wear, has been tested in a research setting in some way. Scientific research in the United States has a rich and sometimes troubling past, but no one will argue that the greatest advances in medicine, for instance, are due to ongoing research efforts.

Research is changing. The web has added an entirely new layer to the research mosaic that involves collecting and analyzing data on Internet behavior. Social networking sites, combined with GIS technology, gather data related to who and *where* our "friends" are. Media research powerhouse A.C. Nielsen recruits families to provide feedback about the shows they watch on TV, and why they like or dislike them. Schools collect and store a wide variety of information on students that is later examined to determine everything from financial aid to roommate assignments. Some research takes place in laboratories, in settings that we can probably imagine (white coats, cold temperatures, metal doors). However, not all research is conducted in this way. Although the sense-making part of research will always require human intervention, the fact is quite a bit of data on a variety of phenomena can now be gathered, analyzed, and disseminated without any human intervention at all.

Libraries have traditionally been seen as service centers, community centers, and learning spaces. They are known to be places where people go to find quiet, to find resources, to find subject experts, to find community. They are not necessarily known as hotbeds of research. In fact, it is quite rare to find a library, regardless of the type, that grounds major service and collection decisions solely on research outcomes. It is not hard to figure out why. In most sectors, research is necessary because the stakes are quite high. Whether it is a public health or medical setting, product marketing, or a political campaign, *not* knowing about the likes, dislikes, habits, opinions, backgrounds, and needs of the public can be quite costly. Libraries do not face the same challenges, so why discuss or write about the need for and application of research in library settings?

Libraries and other information environments continue to face challenges now magnified by the burgeoning technologies that surround us. Library users are changing. Library collections are changing. Library staffs are changing. Even library buildings are changing. As a result of just trying to keep up, it is becoming increasingly difficult for "the library" to define itself moving forward. Many years ago, there was a great deal of discussion about when (not if) the library would become obsolete. The newest neighbor on the block, the Internet, had so much more to offer users, it seemed: convenience, speed, and 24-hour availability. Why bother an actual librarian when Google is easy, fast, and increasingly accurate? Why check out a book when you can read it online, for free? The digital revolution is actually not a revolution; it has settled in to become just another way of life, and libraries are still having a hard time finding their place. Some argue that the main role of the library is to provide access to subject experts—librarians that have a unique and comprehensive knowledge of different subject areas. This is that unique skill that cannot be duplicated by technology (at least, not yet). Others suggest that the library should be a place where rare materials that cannot be made available digitally should be available. Still others wonder if libraries should not just be places for people to gather and find real-world community, as opposed to virtual ones. Libraries actually continue to be all of these things and more, but there is still an uneasy sense that there is something more out there that libraries should be embracing.

Is there any strategy that might help libraries move towards a better-defined, more attuned existence, amidst all of these changes and technological advances? Is there a way to help mitigate the existential crisis that has been brought on by the digital tidal wave? In other sectors, research is used to help define products and services, to test their strengths and weaknesses, to get rid of what does not work. Perhaps the targeted application of research methods to investigate library user needs, user habits, and the user environment, can play a role here. It would not be inaccurate to say that many libraries use surveys and questionnaires routinely to assess user needs.

However, no librarian reading this would disagree that surveys only scratch the surface of what we really want to know about our users. What we are interested in is *understanding* them better—not just asking them if they want extended hours. And understanding users requires a far more in-depth approach than a survey, no matter how comprehensive or well-designed.

To that end, this book is about qualitative research approaches and how they might be applied in library settings to address library and information-specific problems faced by librarians and users. It is not a book about how to conduct a research study; rather, it is a glimpse into some of the ways that user-focused qualitative research, combined with other approaches, might help those who work in libraries find out more about their users, and perhaps generate questions they did not know were out there. There are a number of very well-written books (Wildemuth, 2009; Berg, 2009; Nachimas and Worth-Nachimas, 2008; Denzin and Lincoln, 2000; Miles and Huberman, 1994; see References for Chapter 1 for details) that discuss qualitative research practices in the social sciences in great detail, and this book does not attempt to duplicate those efforts. These books are highly recommended for anyone who wants to learn more about the research process in general.

We can never fully expect to know all there is to know about our users. Although I refer to them here as a single group, they are in fact incredibly heterogeneous, and changing all the time. Each of us is constantly influenced by the world around us, and it will not ever be possible to define, absolutely, the "typical" library user. It is possible, however, to employ a wide variety of creative and interesting information-gathering techniques to learn what we can, and to build on what we already know.

This book has ten chapters. The first chapter provides a definition and very general overview of qualitative research, and some of the approaches that are commonly used.

Chapter 2 takes a look at how qualitative approaches are used in other settings and disciplines to learn more about users, consumers, and patients, and what the library and information world can learn from these applications. Chapter 3 provides an in-depth look at the ethnographic approach, since it has a special relevance for library and information environments. In Chapter 4, I discuss how librarians and others might educate themselves about the relevant areas of research and scholarship that might be germane to their own work settings. The user experience is a very popular topic these days, with lots of discussion about its relevance for library and information settings. Chapter 5 discusses research within the context of examining the user experience. Chapter 6 examines some common library user challenges that might be examined by way of qualitative approaches. The qualitative study of librarians within their own work environment is rare, and Chapter 7 takes a look at ways to evaluate the workplace using qualitative techniques. Libraries operate all over the world, and Chapter 8 explores an example of a global qualitative research project. Librarians do not typically receive formal training as researchers, so Chapter 9 explores some ways in which librarians might learn more about qualitative research. Finally, the last chapter summarizes the message of the book— just do it! All in all, each chapter seeks to shed a little bit of light on how librarians and others might collect and explore qualitative data to learn more about their users, and improve their services. There is no one right way to do this—there are many right ways. Conducting this type of research is often trial and error, but it pays to start somewhere. And every little piece of information that we can learn about our users will only serve to make us all better at what we do in the long run.

Valeda Dent Goodman
November 2010

1

A brief overview of qualitative research

Abstract: This chapter provides general descriptions and definitions for a variety of qualitative research approaches. The chapter is framed by discussion of the anthropological foundations of ethnographic and other qualitative methods.

Key words: qualitative research, observation, qualitative methods, focus groups, interviews, ethnographic research, unobtrusive methods, grounded theory.

This chapter will provide a cursory overview of qualitative research approaches. Keep in mind that this is not meant to be a research manual, or a how-to book, so there are many features that are crucial to the research process that are not discussed. These include constructing a theoretical framework, creating a research design, conducting a literature review, and planning the actual research study. There are a number of good books that cover the research process in its entirety in great detail, including *Designing Qualitative Research* (Marshall and Rossman, 2006); *The Practice of Qualitative Research* (Hesse-Biber and Leavy, 2006); *Handbook of Qualitative Research* (Denzin and Lincoln, 2000); *The Practice of Social Research* (Babbie, 2006); and *Qualitative Research Methods for the Social Sciences* (Berg, 2009).

A description of qualitative research

Qualitative and quantitative approaches to conducting research are often put into two different camps—one that uses numeric data and statistics, and one that uses mostly non-numeric data such as narrative text. Along with this division, there is an unwritten hierarchy in research circles, and quantitative research is considered to be more rigorous, more reliable, and more precise (Berg, 2009, p. 2). In the social sciences, qualitative methods often take a back seat to quantitative approaches. Berg suggests a number of reasons for this, in addition to the ones named above. Qualitative research can often be far more involved, intense work, and produce data that require hours of analysis that cannot be done solely by a software program (Berg, 2009, p. 2). These days, many in the role of teaching research methods emphasize the importance of selecting the correct approach for any given study, as opposed to being loyal to a particular category or design. Research practices that are integrative and combine both qualitative and quantitative activities oftentimes meet the needs of the researcher. Qualitative research can involve statistics and numbers, and quantitative approaches may include narrative descriptions and storytelling. So, at the end of the day, the main goal is to be open-minded in deciding what is most appropriate. The concept of triangulation (Nachimas and Worth-Nachimas, 2008; Wildemuth, 2009; Lee, 1991; Gable, 1994; Mingers, 2001; Ragin, 1987) highlights the importance of using a variety of approaches, depending on the nature of the research.

So how is qualitative research defined? "Qualitative researchers attempt to understand behavior and institutions by getting to know the persons involved and their values, rituals, symbols, beliefs, and emotions" (Nachimas and

Worth-Nachimas, 2008, p. 257). Berg writes that "qualitative research focuses on innovative ways of collecting and analyzing qualitative data collected in natural settings" (2009, p. 2). "Qualitative research refers to the meanings, concepts, definitions, characteristics, metaphors, symbols, and descriptions of things. In contrast, quantitative research refers to counts and measures of things" (Berg, 2009, p. 3). Myers emphasizes understanding as a motivation for conducting qualitative research: "The motivation for doing qualitative research, as opposed to quantitative research, comes from the observation that, if there is one thing which distinguishes humans from the natural world, it is our ability to talk! Qualitative research methods are designed to help researchers understand people and the social and cultural contexts within which they live" (Myers, 2009). Elliot, Fischer and Rennie (1999) offer this definition:

> The aim of qualitative research is to understand and represent the experiences and actions of people as they encounter, engage, and live through situations. In qualitative research, the researcher attempts to develop understandings of the phenomena under study, based as much as possible on the perspective of those being studied. Qualitative researchers accept that it is im-possible to set aside one's own perspective totally (and do not claim to). Nevertheless, they believe that their self-reactive attempts to "bracket" existing theory and their own values allow them to understand and represent their informants' experiences and actions more adequately than would be otherwise possible. (p. 215)

In some texts, participant observation is emphasized as one of the key strategies for collecting qualitative data. In other texts, the practice of ethnographic research and field research are central. There are many variations on the most important elements within the qualitative spectrum, but there is one very central theme that they all share, and that is the importance of meaning. Statistics without context can really only convey so much. Berg (2009) refers to this additional layer of meaning as being related to the "quality of things," by way of words, images, and descriptions (p. 3). Any method that allows the researcher to capture the worlds of others can be a valid qualitative technique.

Gathering the data

There are several methods that can be used to collect data when using a qualitative approach. There are many different strategies, ranging from the popular to the more obscure. Powell (1999) highlights a few, including "phenomenological methods, hermeneutics, ethnomethodology, reflexivity, discourse analysis, and semiotics" (p. 91). One important point to remember about the type of data one chooses to work with is that the data collection technique will often dictate the type of analysis that can be used later to help interpret the data. As well, collecting more than one type of data will allow for a more diverse analysis. These aspects of data collection and the type of research can often be confusing to some. Surveys can yield quantitative data (Likert-scaled responses) that can be statistically analyzed, and they can also produce qualitative data (open-ended textual responses), which may require content analysis. Focus group data, which is normally discussed within the context of qualitative approaches, can be coded and counted, and thus analyzed using statistical methods as well. So, the most important thing to remember when deciding on data collection approaches is matching the research goals and the nature of the research environment to the method.

To illustrate the array of data collection methods that librarians and others may draw from, a few are briefly described below. There are many, many others that researchers should be aware of, which are not covered here. For instance, Carter and Mankoff (2005) explore the use of media in diary studies, since media of all types are an ever-increasing part of everyday life. These approaches are described in the research monographs mentioned at the beginning of this chapter, and discussed in the literature.

Participant observation

Participant observation is a meta-category for a type of data collection strategy that can actually include other techniques such as questionnaires, interviews, and focus groups. Participant observation has a special relevance when it comes to examining library and information service phenomena, as it can be an extension of the normal day-to-day work practices of librarians. Librarians typically spend at least some portion of their day actively engaged with users, participating to some extent in the users' research activities by assisting them with instruction and reference. In this way, they are already participants, and observers, in the users' environment.

Anthropologists have been long familiar with participant observation; noted anthropologist Malinowski (1922, p. 7) talked about his research in the Omarkana Trobriand Islands in the South Pacific:

> As I went on my morning walk through the village, I could see intimate details of family life, of toilet, cooking, taking of meals; I could see the arrangements

for the day's work, people starting on their errands, or groups of men and women busy at some manufacturing tasks. Quarrels, jokes, family scenes, events usually trivial, sometimes dramatic but always significant, form the atmosphere of my daily life, as well as theirs.

Jorgensen (1989) describes participant observation this way:

The methodology of participant observation is appropriate for studies of almost every aspect of human existence. Through participant observation, it is possible to describe what goes on, who or what is involved, when and where things happen, how they occur, and why—at least from the standpoints of participants. The methodology of participant observation is exceptional for studying processes, relationships among people and events, the organization of people and events, continuities over time, and patterns, as well as the immediate sociocultural contexts in which human existence unfolds. (p. 12)

Jorgensen goes on to describe several situations where one might consider using participant observation (1989, p. 12):

- Little is known about the phenomenon.
- There are important differences between the views of insiders as opposed to outsiders.
- The phenomenon is somehow obscured from the view of outsiders.
- The phenomenon is hidden from public view.

DeWalt and DeWalt (2002) suggest that participation observation is most useful when researchers want to understand both explicit (behaviors, thoughts, actions, and practices that are easy to articulate) and tacit (thoughts, norms, and practices that may not be a part of our conscious awareness) phenomena within a culture. Participant observation is seen by many as one of the hallmarks of cultural exploration within the field of cultural anthropology (DeWalt and DeWalt, 2002), and one of the foundations for ethnographic approaches to research (Schensul, 1999). Specifically, participant observation goes beyond just watching what people do and say—it also includes the rigorous recording of the researcher's experience, and the analysis and interpretation of this documentation. While participant observation is standard in many anthropological field research settings, its application is rare within information and library settings (Cooper, Lewis and Urquhart, 2004). Why might this be the case, especially when library and information environments seem the perfect place to observe user behavior? The challenges are some of the same faced by the application of qualitative approaches in general—the amount of time, human resources, and attention to detail required is extremely high, and far greater than most librarians or information professionals have the time to devote to.

Focus groups

Focus groups are very familiar to anyone who has dabbled in research, and are frequently used within library and information service settings to gather data on a specific topic. Focus groups provide a way to collect data, and include the use of carefully selected groups of people that come together to discuss specific questions or issues related to some research question or phenomenon. Interaction is key, and one of the more distinctive characteristics of the focus group is the ability of group members to share their thoughts and ideas in a group setting, as opposed to in a one-on-one interview.

According to Wildemuth (2009), this interaction can lead to "a more nuanced perspective on a topic than could have been discovered through individual interviews" (p. 242). The benefits of this approach include the value of actually hearing and experiencing the thoughts and feelings of group members expressed in person as opposed to unilateral, non-interactive collection methods such as surveys. There are certainly limitations to using focus groups, including those related to the transcription of the sessions and to confidentiality. The focus group moderator must be carefully chosen, and may not always be the principal investigator. Sample size, recruiting of participants, and videorecording of the groups are also issues that have to be carefully addressed before the group convenes. As well, making sure that the group stays on task in terms of discussing the issue is important. Focus groups can be paired with other data collection techniques such as questionnaires, usability tests, think-alouds, and interviews.

Interviews

Interviews are widely used as a way to gather information from study participants. Berg (2009) cites three different types of interviews: standardized, semistructured, and unstructured (p. 105). Berg further defines interviewing as "a conversation with a purpose" (p. 101). There are many different elements to the interview, and although there is no one right way to conduct interviews, most researchers would agree that it is a cross between an art and a skill, and it takes time to learn to do it well. Interviews can be done over the phone, in person, and, increasingly, over the web using such applications as Skype, instant messaging, and chat (Opdenakker, 2006). Regardless of the type of interview, this approach can provide first-person accounts and feedback that can be difficult to gather any other way. Hutchinson, Wilson and Wilson (1994, p. 161) suggest that "catharsis, self-acknowledgement, sense of purpose, self-awareness, empowerment, healing, and providing a voice for the disenfranchised" can all be seen as "unanticipated benefits" of interviews. Interviews can also be combined with other data collection methods for more diverse data coverage.

Case studies

The case study is an approach that features the intense examination of a particular "unit of analysis" (Trochim, 2006). Organizations, individuals in certain settings, or events can be explored via case study (Wildemuth, 2009, p. 53). The case study can yield qualitative or quantitative data, and like focus groups, can have other data collection strategies embedded within such as interviews, questionnaires, participant observation, and think-alouds. A case study of an organization may, for instance, include a survey with data that is subject to further statistical analysis. Wildemuth (2009, p. 52) suggests that there are four questions that should be asked to determine whether the case study is a good research approach:

- Does the phenomenon of interest have to be studied in a natural setting?
- Does the phenomenon of interest focus on contemporary events?
- Does the research question aim to answer how and why questions?
- Does the phenomenon of interest include a variety of factors and relationships that can be directly observed?

Within library and information settings, case studies might explore attitudes and work practices of staff over a certain period of time, or the research habits of a cohort of doctoral students within a department.

Exploring stories and narratives

Narratives and storytelling provide yet another way for researchers to gather rich, personal, qualitative data. Stories and narratives have many functions within any given culture and the greater society, and these practices may play out differently in oral and literate cultures. Oftentimes, in literate cultures, stories are read from or at least associated with a text. In cultures that are primarily oral, there is no written text to draw from, and memory serves as the place where these stories are kept for retelling: "Of all verbal genres, narrative has the most evident and straightforward relationship to memory" (Ong, 1982, p. 12). Ong reminds the reader that stories in oral cultures may not necessarily proceed in the same order that we are used to, although there is always some kind of storyline (1982, p. 19); "Oral narrative is not much concerned with exact sequential parallelism, which becomes an objective of the mind possessed by literacy" (p. 19). According to Koch (1998), "stories can be therapeutic"; "stories can inform social policy"; "stories can facilitate change in organizations"; "stories can allow marginalized groups to have a voice" (p. 1183). Bamberg (1997) suggests that stories help to create a moral order, and Bruner (1991) explicates the value of the narrative in sharing morals and values. Stories play a role in religion, history, development of cultures and the self, and are frequently shared between adult and child. "The practice of giving our children moral lessons in the form of stories is common not only in western traditions, but in many, perhaps most, other cultures" (Walton and Brewer, 2001, p. 308).

Researchers illustrate the various distinctions between the story and the narrative, although it can sometimes be hard to differentiate the two. Labov (1972) defines the narrative as a discourse of related events told in an organized manner. These events can be real or not. Labov and Waletsky (1997) articulate in painstaking detail the components of the personal narrative by identifying its structural components. The authors were particularly concerned with differences in class and race (p. 5) and examined sequence, grammatical structure, and social context of the narrators during the course of their study. Mischler (1995) discusses a typology for narrative analysis with three possible perspectives from which to evaluate the narrative: reference and temporal order, textual coherence and structure, and narrative functions (p. 90). Mischler also used Halliday's (1973) well-known model of language function to classify narrative approaches (Mischler, 1995, p. 89). Richardson (1997) suggests that narratives are both "a means of knowing and a method of telling" (p. 58).

Heath (1986) defines the narrative as "verbalized memories of past or ongoing experiences" (p. 84). Heath suggests that narratives exist in all societies, that these narratives are produced in predictable ways, and that they can be shared in oral or written form (p. 85). Heath clarifies that, while the narrative and the story are sometimes synonymous, there are cultures where fictional narratives are rare (p. 85). Heath's (1986) research in this area focuses on the social context for language learning, and connecting language and the study of the narrative to the role of adults in children's daily lives; the goals adults have for their children's futures; and the connections of adults and children to schools and other community organizations (p. 85). According to Heath

(1986), there are four universal types of narratives: recounts, eventcasts, accounts, and stories. Recounts feature "experiences of the past in which the speaker had one of several possible roles" (Heath, 1986, p. 88). The eventcast is a "verbal replay or explanation of activity scenes that are either in the current attention of those participating in the eventcast or are being planned for the future" (p. 88). The account involves the teller sharing what they have experienced. The last genre, the story, may also be a retelling of events, but with far more structure. Stories may also contain more fictional elements, and language use beyond what would be expected in everyday use (p. 89).

Researchers frequently develop typologies or frameworks to better understand and interpret stories or narratives. Lieblich, Tuval-Mashiach and Zibler (1998) defined four models for interpretation: holistic-content, holistic-form, categorical-content, and categorical-form. Mischler (1986) also discusses ways to analyze the narrative. Keats (2009) discusses the ability of the researcher to deepen their understanding of the participant's narratives by examining multiple texts, including the visual, the written and the spoken (p. 188).

Any given library may contain thousands of stories. Every user and every employee is a potential storyteller. Moreover, library artifacts such as books, computers, and desks also tell us stories about their own use, in some way. Deciding whether to solicit narratives for a particular research endeavor depends on the research question. A staff member who has been employed by the library in a variety of positions and over a long period of time may provide a very interesting narrative that converges with modern-day changes in service and user populations. Such a narrative, or a group of similar narratives, may help to focus in on the elements within the library that have *not* changed much, and that need further exploration. The narrative is a great complement to other data that may not convey the same level of personal detail, but it can be time-consuming and complicated in terms of coding and analysis.

Unobtrusive methods

So far, all of the methods discussed above require the active participation of the subject, whether that means participating in a focus group or an interview, or taking a survey. These methods all intrude upon the participants in some way, and necessitate their being engaged in the research process. There are a number of methods for collecting data that do not require the active participation of subjects, known as unobtrusive data collection techniques. Berg (2009) suggests that unobtrusive methods examine the "traces people either intentionally or inadvertently leave behind" (p. 269). Unobtrusive techniques include, but are not limited to, the examination of archival and historical data and artifacts, census records, vital records such as birth, marriage, and death certificates, and written accounts such as diaries, biographies, and autobiographies. These days, data collected from internet use—for instance, which sites people visit, which sites get the most referrals from web searches, and which advertisements generate the most traffic—all generate data that can be explored to learn more about Internet users without the solicited participation of the user. GIS data are also being used increasingly to map location and personal activity on many levels, sometimes without the awareness of the individual. Furthermore, personal artifacts and those things that are left behind can tell a story about the behavior or experience of people or groups, and can be explored using behavior trace or physical trace observation (Berg, 2009). The best known study of this type is the

Tucson Garbage Study, which was initiated in 1973 by Dr William Rathje at the University of Arizona (Berg, 2009). Over the past 30 years, Dr Rathje and his colleagues and students have sifted through and classified the contents of "more than 14 tons of excavated material" (Rybczynski, 1992) from local garbage dumps. The idea is that garbage can tell us a lot about people's lifestyles and behaviors. In a physical library setting, water bottles in garbage cans, reorganized furniture, and circulation records can tell us a lot about users' habits and behaviors, and lead to further exploration. There is no limit to the type of information that may actually yield useful data about different phenomena, groups, or individuals.

A little bit about grounded theory

I am devoting a separate section to this topic because it is a potentially valuable approach to consider within the framework of library-related research. In 1967, Glaser and Strauss published *The Discovery of Grounded Theory*. Some tend to associate qualitative research in general with the generation of hypotheses (rather than hypothesis testing), but this is a false distinction. Grounded theory simply represents one way to generate theory from data, and make sense of qualitative data that are textual in nature. All qualitative research does not necessarily use a grounded theory approach.

Grounded theory allows researchers to generate hypotheses after data collection, and after careful examination of the data (Auerbach and Silverstein, 2003). The method has two main principles: questioning rather than measuring, and hypotheses generation using theoretical coding (Auerbach and Silverstein, 2003, p. 7). The "grounding" of theory thus first takes place in relation to the actual data. Glaser and Strauss (1967) state that grounded theory is the discovery of theory from data systematically obtained from social research (p. 3), and that this method is the best way to generate theory that is "suited to its supposed uses" (p. 3). The discovery of categories from the data is one of the strengths of the approach because the origins are clear (Glaser and Strauss, 1967).

One of the most critical steps in this process is the coding of the data, which in the case of this study will be inductive in nature, and facilitated by a qualitative content analysis. Auerbach and Silverstein (2003, p. 35) discuss the seven elements in the grounded theory coding process:

- Raw text
- Relevant text
- Repeating ideas
- Themes
- Theoretical constructs
- Theoretical narrative
- Research concerns.

These steps progress from the most elementary to the most sophisticated, with the first step being the initial examination of the raw text. The development of the theoretical constructs are key to surfacing the research concerns or questions. It should be noted that the process of coding the data is iterative, not linear, in nature (Auerbach and Silverstein, 2003, p. 43).

Grounded theory approaches can be extremely time-consuming and involved. Moreover, it can be difficult to determine reliability and validity. To this end, Silverstein et al. (2006) suggest that transferability, and not generalizability, should be one of the guidelines for evaluating qualitative research. Transferability is facilitated in part by the researchers providing great detail about the researchers themselves, the participants, the context, and "the dynamic interaction between researcher and participants" (Silverstein et al., 2006, p. 352). Given the limitations, there may still be instances within library settings where grounded theory approaches are warranted, especially when trying to understand more about why a particular phenomenon may be occurring.

A little bit about analyzing the data

If the data collection method involves the collection of textual content, it has to be analyzed and made sense of in some way in order to be useful. This content—whether transcripts from focus groups, interviews, oral histories, or videotaped storytelling sessions—has to be "decoded" so it can be summarized and understood by others. Content analysis provides a way to do this. Although this is not the only technique for textual analysis, it is a major one. It is in this type of analysis that the most striking differences between quantitative and qualitative approaches can be seen.

According to Berg (2009), content analysis is a "careful, detailed, systematic examination and interpretation of a particular body of material in an effort to identify patterns, themes, biases, and meanings" (p. 338). Berg goes on to suggest that content analysis has been used in many different disciplines, including psychology, education, business, sociology, political science, art, and others, and that it is "chiefly a coding operation and data interpretation process" (p. 339). Wildemuth (2009) clarifies the difference between content analysis and qualitative content analysis, suggesting that the latter "goes beyond merely counting words or extracting objective content from text to examine meanings, themes, and patterns that may be manifest or latent in a particular text" (p. 309).

The content itself can be represented by interview transcripts, survey responses, focus groups, print media such as books and newspapers, or observations, and be verbal, print, or electronic in its format (Kondracki and Wellman, 2002). A number of researchers have discussed the application of this qualitative approach, including Wildemuth (2006), Cavanagh (1997), Babbie (2006), Miles and Huberman (1994), Glaser and Strauss (1967), Budd et al. (1967), Downe-Wamboldt (1992), Lincoln and Guba (1985), and many others. Downe-Wamboldt (1992, p. 314) states that content analysis is meant to provide "knowledge and understanding" of the situation being studied. Content analysis was first used as early as the eighteenth century for data analysis (Barcus, 1959), and, although the approach is mostly seen as a qualitative one, it has also been applied as a quantitative approach (Morgan, 1993).

Hsieh and Shannon (2005) define three clear and succinct categories for the application of content analysis: conventional content analysis, directed content analysis, and summative content analysis (p. 1277). Conventional content analysis is a way to describe a phenomenon when the existing information or theory on its occurrence is limited (Hsieh and Shannon, 2005, p. 1279). Researchers examine the text, and allow names for categories to emerge from the text, as opposed to assigning pre-determined categories (p. 1279). Directed content analysis is less flexible in terms of identifying key themes and categories. This approach begins with the assumption that existing theory is helpful, and can be used to explain a phenomenon, but it is incomplete. Researchers use this approach to "validate or extend" current theory (p. 1281). Thus, categories are pre-determined from the existing literature, as opposed to surfacing from the textual examination. For instance, Maslow's (1943) hierarchy of needs may serve as pre-set categories from which to code open-ended questions about college students' adjustment experiences in college.

The last category that Hsieh and Shannon (2005) discuss is the summative content analysis approach. This approach has two distinct stages. First, certain content or words in the text are identified and quantified, in an effort to better understand their context and use within the text (2005, p. 1283). The second step involves what Holsti (1969) refers to as latent content analysis, that is, the interpretation of the words in the text with the purpose of discovering their underlying meaning (Hsieh and Shannon, 2005, p. 1284). Summative analysis connects the frequency of a given word with its contextual meaning, and also aims to deepen the understanding of the phenomenon by the researcher. Meanings associated with different words, related symbolism, and euphemistic versus explicit meaning are all areas where the researcher may discover rich connections and meaning associated with the text (Hsieh and Shannon, 2005).

Challenges to working with qualitative data

There are several limitations to the use of qualitative data discussed in the literature (Berg, 2009; Marshall and Rossman, 2006; Barbour, 2001; Hesse-Biber and Leavy, 2006). As a result, researchers from various disciplines have long struggled to better define what makes a good qualitative study (Stiles, 1993; Guba and Lincoln, 1989; Miles and Huberman, 1984; Mischler, 1986; Rennie, 1999; Barbour, 2001; Seale and Silverman, 1997). A must-read for any librarian interested in qualitative research is Sandstrom and Sandstrom (1995), which highlights the (sometimes misguided) application of anthropologic methods within Library and Information Studies research, and offers some suggestions for improving these practices (see Chapter 3 for more on Sandstrom and Sandstrom).

Elliot et al. (1999) propose a set of "evolving guidelines" for the review of qualitative research in order "to contribute to the process of legitimizing qualitative research; to ensure more appropriate and valid scientific reviews of qualitative manuscripts, theses, and dissertations; to encourage better quality control in qualitative research through better self- and other-monitoring; and to encourage further developments in approach and method" (Elliot et al., 1999, p. 215).

Sandelowski (1986) addresses the problem of rigor in qualitative approaches, another reason why researchers may be hesitant to invest time and effort in its application. The author suggests that "four factors complicate the debate about the scientific merits of qualitative research: the varieties of qualitative methods, the lack of clear boundaries between quantitative and qualitative research, the tendency to evaluate qualitative research against conventional scientific criteria of rigor, and the artistic features of qualitative inquiry" (1986, p. 27).

Barbour (2001, p. 1116) provides a checklist of five "technical fixes" that researchers can employ to improve the quality control aspects of qualitative work. The author suggests that purposive sampling can address bias; the use of grounded theory can address the creation of original theories; multiple coders can address inter-rater reliability;

triangulation can address internal validity; and respondent validation can address the interpretations being made by the researchers.

Particular data collection methods have drawbacks, as well. For instance, Potter and Hepburn (2005) explain the types of problems that can be encountered during the interview and the subsequent reporting of the interview: "(1) the deletion of the interviewer; (2) the conventions for representing interaction; (3) the specificity of analytic observations; (4) the unavailability of the interview set-up; (5) the failure to consider interviews as interaction" (p. 281).

The most important thing for librarians is to be aware of the limitations of whatever method they choose, and how those limitations might impact the research process and the outcomes. Librarians can also employ multiple methods to collect data—such as the aforementioned triangulation (Ragin, 1987; Kaplan and Duchon, 1988; Mingers, 2001; Wildemuth, 2009), thus eliminating the reliance on just one type of collection technique.

References

Auerbach, C.F. and Silverstein, L.B. (2003) *Qualitative Data: An Introduction to Coding and Analysis*. New York: New York University Press.

Babbie, E. (2006) *The Practice of Social Research*. New York: Macmillan.

Bamberg, M. (1997) A constructivist approach to narrative development. In M. Bamberg (ed.), *Narrative development: Six approaches* (pp. 89–132). Mahwah, NJ: Erlbaum.

Barbour, R.S. (2001) Checklists for improving rigour in qualitative research: A case of the tail wagging the dog? *British Medical Journal*, 322(7294): 1115–17.

Barcus, F.E. (1959) Communications content: analysis of the research 1900–1958 (a content analysis of content analysis). Unpublished doctoral dissertation, University of Illinois, Urbana-Champaign.

Berg, B. (2009) *Qualitative research methods for the social sciences*, 7th edition. Boston, MA: Allyn and Bacon.

Bruner, J. (1991) The narrative construction of reality. *Critical Inquiry*, 18(1): 1–21.

Budd, R.W., Thorp, R.K. and Donohew, L. (1967) *Content analysis of communications*. New York, NY: Macmillan.

Carter, S. and Mankoff, J. (2005) When participants do the capturing: the role of media in diary studies. *Conference on Human Factors in Computing Systems, Proceedings of the SIGCHI Conference on Human Factors in Computing Systems*, 899–908.

Cavanagh, S. (1997) Content analysis: concepts, methods and applications. *Nurse Researcher*, 4(3): 5–16.

Cooper, J., Lewis, R. and Urquhart, C. (2004) Using participant or non-participant observation to explain information behaviour. *Information Research*, 9(4). Retrieved from *http://informationr.net/ir/9-4/paper184.html*.

Denzin, N. and Lincoln, Y. (2000) *Handbook of Qualitative Research*. Thousand Oaks, CA: Sage.

DeWalt, K.M. and DeWalt, B.R. (2002) *Participant Observation: A Guide for Fieldworkers*. Walnut Creek, CA: Altamira Press.

Downe-Wamboldt, B. (1992) Content analysis: Method, applications, and issues. *Health Care for Women International*, 13: 313–21.

Elliott, R., Fischer, C.T. and Rennie, D.L. (1999) Evolving guidelines for publication of qualitative research studies in psychology and related fields. *British Journal of Clinical Psychology*, 38(3): 215–29.

Gable, G. (1994) Integrating case study and survey research methods: An example in information systems. *European Journal of Information Systems*, 3(2): 112–26.

Glaser, B.G. and Strauss, A.L. (1967) *The Discovery of Grounded Theory: Strategies for Qualitative Research.* Chicago, IL: Aldine Publishing Company.

Guba, E.G. and Lincoln, Y.S. (1989) Judging the quality of fourth generation evaluation. In E.G. Guba and Y. Lincoln (eds), *Fourth Generation Evaluation.* Newbury Park, CA: Sage (pp. 228–251).

Halliday, M.A.K. (1973) *Explorations in the Functions of Language.* London: Edward Arnold.

Heath, S.B. (1986) Taking a cross-cultural look at narratives. In F. Kuecker (ed.), *Topics in Language Disorders* (pp. 84–94). Rockville, MD: Aspen Publishers.

Holsti, O.R. (1969) *Content Analysis for the Social Sciences and Humanities.* Reading, MA: Addison-Wesley.

Hsieh, H. and Shannon, S.E. (2005) Three approaches to qualitative content analysis. *Qualitative Health Research*, 15(9): 1277–88.

Hutchinson, S.A., Wilson, M.E. and Wilson, H.S. (1994) Benefits of participating in research interviews. *Journal of Nursing Scholarship*, 26(2): 161–6.

Jorgensen, D. (1989) *Participant Observation: A Methodology for Human Studies.* Thousand Oaks, CA: Sage.

Kaplan, B. and Duchon, D. (1988) Combining qualitative and quantitative methods in information systems research: A case study. *MIS Quarterly*, 12(4): 571–86.

Keats, P. (2009) Multiple text analysis in narrative research: Visual, written, and spoken stories of experience. *Qualitative Research*, 9(2): 181–95.

Koch, T. (1998) Storytelling: Is it really research? *Journal of Advanced Nursing*, 28(6): 1182–90.

Kondracki, N.L. and Wellman, N.S. (2002) Content analysis: Review of methods and their applications in nutrition education. *Journal of Nutrition Education and Behavior*, 34: 224–30.

Labov, W. (1972) *Sociolinguistic Patterns*. Philadelphia, PA: University of Pennsylvania Press.

Labov, W. and Waletzky, J. (1997) Narrative analysis: Oral versions of personal experience. *Journal of Narrative Life and History*, 7(1–4): 3–38.

Lee, A. (1991) Integrating positivist and interpretive approaches to organizational research. *Organization Science*, 2(4): 342–65.

Lieblich, A., Tuval-Mashiach, R. and Zibler, T. (1998) *Narrative Research: Reading, Analysis, and Interpretation*. Newbury Park, CA: Sage.

Lincoln, Y.S. and Guba, E.G. (1985) *Naturalistic Inquiry*. Beverly Hills, CA: Sage.

Malinowski, B. (1922) *Argonauts of the Western Pacific. An Account of Native Enterprise and Adventure in the Archipelagos of Melanesian New Guinea*. London, UK: George Routledge.

Marshall, C. and Rossman, G. (2006) *Designing Qualitative Research*. Thousand Oaks, CA: Sage.

Maslow, A.H. (1943) A theory of human motivation. *Psychological Review*, 50(4): 370–96.

Miles, M. and Huberman, A.M. (1984) *Qualitative Data Analysis: A Sourcebook of New Methods*, 1st edition. Newbury Park, CA: Sage Publications.

Miles, M. and Huberman, A.M. (1994) *Qualitative Data Analysis*. Thousand Oaks, CA: Sage.

Mingers, J. (2001) Combining IS research methods: Towards a pluralist methodology. *Information Systems Research*, 12(3): 240–59.

Mischler, E. (1986) *Research Interviewing: Context and Narrative*. Cambridge, MA: Harvard University Press.

Mischler, E. (1995) Models of narrative analysis: A typology. *Journal of Narrative and Life History*, 5(2): 87–123.

Morgan, D.L. (1993) Qualitative content analysis: A guide to paths not taken. *Qualitative Health Research*, 3: 112–21.

Myers, M.D. (2009) Association for Information Systems qualitative research in information systems. Retrieved from *http://www.qual.auckland.ac.nz/*.

Nachimas, D. and Worth-Nachimas, C. (2008) *Research Methods in the Social Sciences*, 7th edition. New York: Worth Publishers.

Nagy Hesse-Biber, S. and Leavy, P. (2006) *The Practice of Qualitative Research*. Thousand Oaks, CA: Sage.

Ong, W. (1982) Oral remembering and narrative structures. In D. Tannen (ed.), *Georgetown University roundtable on language and linguistics 1981, Analyzing discourse: Text and talk* (pp. 12–24) Washington, DC: Georgetown University Press.

Opdenakker, R. (2006) Advantages and disadvantages of four interview techniques. *Qualitative Research Journal*, 7(4). Retrieved from *http://www.qualitative-research.net/index.php/fqs/article/view/175*.

Potter, J. and Hepburn, A. (2005) Qualitative interviews in psychology: Problems and possibilities. *Qualitative Research in Psychology*, 22(4): 281–307.

Powell, R. (1999) Recent trends in research: A methodological essay. *Library and Information Science Research*, 21(1): 91–119.

Ragin, C.C. (1987) *The Comparative Method: Moving Beyond Qualitative and Quantitative Strategies*. Berkeley, CA: University of California Press.

Rennie, D.L. (1999) Qualitative research: A matter of hermeneutics and the sociology of knowledge. In

M. Kopala and L.A. Suzuki (eds), *Using qualitative methods in psychology* (pp. 3–14). Thousand Oaks, CA: Sage.

Richardson, L. (1997) *Fields of Play: Constructing an Academic Life*. New Brunswick, NJ: Rutgers University Press.

Rybczynski, W. (1992) We are what we throw away. Retrieved from *http://www.nytimes.com/1992/07/05/books/we-are-what-we-throw-away.html?pagewanted=1*.

Sandelowski, M. (1986) The problem of rigor in qualitative research. *Advances in Nursing Science*, 8(3): 27–37.

Sandstrom, A. and Sandstrom, P. (1995) The use and misuse of anthropological methods in library and information science research. *Library Quarterly*, 65(2): 161–99.

Schensul, J.J. (1999) Building community research partnerships in the struggle against AIDS. *Health Education and Behavior*, 26(2): 266–83.

Seale, C. and Silverman, D. (1997) Ensuring rigour in qualitative research. *European Journal of Public Health*, 7: 379–84.

Silverstein, L. Auerbach, C. and Levant, R. (2006) Using qualitative research to strengthen clinical practice. *Professional Psychology: Research and Practice*, 37(4): 351–8.

Stiles, W.B. (1993) Quality control in qualitative research. *Clinical Psychology Review*, 13: 593–618.

Trochim, W. (2006) *Research Methods: The Concise Knowledge Base*. London: Atomic Dog Publications.

Walton, M. and Brewer, C. (2001) The role of personal narrative in bringing children into the moral discourse of their culture. *Narrative Inquiry*, 11(2): 307–34.

Wildemuth, B. (2006) Evidence-based practice in search interface design. *Journal of the American Society for Information Science and Technology*, 57(6): 825–8.

Wildemuth, B. (ed.) (2009) *Applications of Social Research Methods to Questions in Information and Library Science*. Westport, CN: Libraries Unlimited.

2

Examples of qualitative research in non-library settings

Abstract: This chapter explores several examples of qualitative work in other settings, including the entertainment field, nursing, and academia.

Key words: A.C. Nielsen, qualitative nursing research, ethnographic research of students, student habits.

Librarians and others interested in discovering how users work and what they need can learn a lot from the practice and application of qualitative research in other areas. This chapter will briefly review just a few examples of novel qualitative approaches from the academic, nursing/medical, and media industries.

Becoming a student: research in an academic environment

In the spring of 2002, Professor Cathy Small, an anthropology professor at Northern Arizona University, applied, as a student, to a university. She was accepted. She did not apply because she wanted to return to school; it was because she wanted to gain a better understanding of what college life means in this day and age. Her approach was as a participant observer in the truest sense of the word: "I opted for a more daily immersion, in which I actually took courses, lived in the dorms, and encountered students as an older but fellow student" (Nathan, 2005, p. 5). Her book, *My Freshman Year: What a Professor Learned by Becoming a Student*, is a wonderfully crafted retelling of her time as a student, and the insights she gained into American student life. It is clear by the end of the book that without complete immersion in student culture it would have been impossible to capture all of the nuances associated with this unique environment. Small's data collection during her time as a college student included focus groups, interviews, activity diaries, observation (for instance, monitoring of eating/seating arrangements in the college cafeteria), a dorm activity log, and a survey of informal conversation topics (Nathan, 2005, p. 15).

Although Small's approach was novel, and unusual, using ethnographic approaches to study students within the context of higher education is not a recent development. In 1989, Michael Moffatt wrote *Coming of Age in New Jersey: College and American Culture*. This book is frequently referenced as one of the premier studies of American college life. Moffatt, an anthropologist, did not "become" a student—he studied students in the more traditional sense to pen this interesting ethnography. Around that same time, Helen Lefkowitz-Horowitz published *Campus life: Undergraduate Cultures from the End of the Eighteenth Century to the Present* (1988); Barbara Miller Solomon wrote *In the Company of Educated Women: A History of Women and Higher Education* (1985) and Averil McClelland wrote *The Education of Women in the United States* (1992). Certainly, these ethnographic writings were and still are of great value in learning more about college and university student culture.

A.C. Nielsen Company as an example of rich media research

Within business settings, market research is often the key to understanding ways to improve profit. One of the more interesting examples of a research-driven industry is the entertainment industry—specifically, broadcast and cable television, and web-based, on-demand, and mobile entertainment. In the United States, people may be familiar with the A.C. Nielsen Company, perhaps the best-known marketing and audience measurement firm in the world. The company was started in 1936 by Arthur Nielsen, an engineer, with the initial creation of the Nielsen Food and Drug Indices, which provided sales data. The Nielsen ratings box, first known as the Audiometer (Nielsen, 2010), was later procured by Nielsen and used to record radio and television viewing statistics. At present, Nielsen provides market and research data on everything from broadcast and cable television to consumer internet behavior to mobile device use. Their strength, according to the company website, is the provision of data to help businesses understand the customer better, and in turn create better products (Nielsen, 2010). The company emphasizes the connection between understanding user behavior and profit. They also emphasize the idea of segmentation—all products and services are not created equal—and their research illustrates this (Nielsen, 2010). The company has several methods for collecting and sharing data related to "mobile consumer behaviors, attitudes and experiences" (Nielsen, 2010), including:

- mobile subscriber counts
- bill panel
- drive tests

- on-device meters
- online surveys
- mobile application testing

The other research areas of focus are mobile devices, wireless, Internet, radio, and something the company calls "three screens," which is described as program-watching "via the Internet and on cell phones, in-home and out-of-home, live and time-shifted, free and paid, rebroadcasts and original program streams" (Nielsen, 2010). According to their website, Nielsen measures 40 percent of the world's television (Nielsen, 2010). Measurement for television viewing includes electronic metering technology—which features two types of in-home meters. The set meters "capture what channel is being tuned," and the People Meters "gather information about who is watching" (Nielsen, 2010). Diaries, one way to collect qualitative data, may also be used in some homes selected as samples for viewers to record additional information about what they are watching. These various data are collected in a large database, which subscribers access to examine valuable information about the preferences and viewing habits of viewers. The television ratings that Nielsen publishes are a way to express how TV shows fare in certain markets, with certain demographics, in certain time slots, and against other shows. These TV ratings play a major role in the decision-making process for broadcast television, cable, and internet TV in terms of which shows will be renewed or cancelled, and even more importantly, which content will be the most lucrative in terms of advertising.

Nielsen is also in the business of consumer research: "Nielsen measures product sales, market share, distribution, price and merchandising conditions in tens of thousands of retail outlets such as grocery stores, drug stores, mass merchandisers and convenience stores" (Nielsen, 2010). This means that broadcasters are able to connect television programming, product commercials, and buying habits using Nielsen data. Certainly, this level of detailed and targeted research is far beyond the scope of what any library needs, but it provides an interesting lens through which to view the role of research in today's consumer and technology-driven culture. Nielsen capitalizes on the fact that patterns and habits are connected to the type of experiences users prefer, and data can highlight this interconnectedness. These data have great value—the fees that companies pay to access Nielsen datasets are a testament to that fact.

Knowing a little bit about what Nielsen does, one might think: Well, why not have a Nielsen-type data-mining outfit for libraries, based on all sorts of user data that would be continuously collected and mined? If one looks at libraries in subsets, for instance, all the libraries in the United States, one of the major constraints that libraries have in terms of understanding user patterns and behaviors is the fact that libraries very seldom share the data that they do have and collect, with other libraries. Certainly, users are very different from one another, whether they are using the same library or using libraries across the country. On the other hand, Nielsen captures data from incredibly diverse samples, and, despite the fact that those television watchers are very different people, similar patterns tend to emerge. A number of research studies have investigated the impact of the Internet on information-seeking behavior of users. If, as Nielsen suggests, users are now "three-screen" savvy—that is, they look for information and access media and entertainment on their mobile devices, television sets, and their computers—it stands to reason that there is also within this matrix a place where physical and virtual library spaces also play a role. One could ask, how do the changing mobile behaviors of users impact their library use? Or changing Internet behavior? Or television viewing? There are some very intriguing questions out there. One thing is for certain: the environments (virtual or physical) that users operate in are becoming less important, while their preferences and habits become more so.

Qualitative research in nursing

Nursing is one area that has embraced the application of qualitative research to understand patients, patient care, treatment environments, administrative matters, and psychological concerns related to healthcare. A review of the nursing research literature reveals numerous examples of qualitative research studies (Holloway and Wheeler, 2002; Bowling, 2002; Greenhalgh and Taylor, 1997; Brookes, 2007; Munhall and Oiler-Boyd, 1997; Streubert and Carpenter, 2010). The primary objective in using qualitative approaches in the field has less to do with proving cause and effect, and more to do with investigating patient experiences. "Qualitative approaches are necessary in primary healthcare when researchers want to ask questions about behaviour and to focus on participants' experiences" (Brookes, 2007, p. 32). The use of qualitative approaches in nursing has been met with the same skepticism at times as has its use in other disciplines, mainly based on the belief that qualitative research is inherently less rigorous (Sandelowski, 1986) and less reliable than its quantitative counterpart. Regardless of this, the literature provides a variety of studies which have used qualitative approaches successfully. A good example is a study done by Sharif and Masoumi (2005). The researchers investigated nursing students' experiences of their clinical practice activities. Focus groups were used to collect data from a subject pool of 90 students, and the data reviewed and coded for patterns and themes. Four themes emerged that were deemed as being important components of the students' clinical experience: initial clinical anxiety, theory-practice gap, clinical supervision, and professional role (Sharif and Masoumi, 2005). Collecting and coding data from focus groups is a common qualitative approach, and can often be combined with other methods to provide a more comprehensive picture of the phenomenon being studied. In Spoelstra and Robbins (2010), the researchers examined the transition from registered nurse to advanced practicing nurse by collecting data from nursing students enrolled in an online course. A qualitative thematic analysis (Spoelstra and Robbins, 2010) produced both important themes and sub-themes that highlighted the students' feelings about making this transition. The insight provided by way of the students' thoughts and ideas about this transition was greatly facilitated by the use of open-ended questions and dialogue.

Nurses deal with a diversity of patients, diagnoses, and situations in their work, and it can be difficult to capture these experiences and make sense of them so that they can be shared to improve and understand the demanding role of the nurse in patient care. A number of studies have used qualitative strategies to explore the perceptions of nurses about the work they do. Georges et al. (2002) collected qualitative data to explore nurses' perceptions about their work on a palliative care ward. Kerr (2002) observed and videotaped nurses' shift handover practices, then coded and studied the data to determine best practices, and the resulting areas for improvement. Owen (1989) explored the role of hope in severely ill cancer patients by "eliciting vivid descriptions of hopeful cancer patients from clinical nurse specialists" (Owen, 1989, p. 75). This process allowed the researcher to then develop sub-themes from the contextual analysis, followed by a conceptual model of hope (Owen, 1989).

The nursing literature provides just a glimpse of the many ways qualitative approaches can be utilized within a field to explore complex phenomena and foster greater understanding between practitioners, patients, and organizations.

Qualitative research in medicine and mental health disciplines

Qualitative studies are frequently found in the medical and mental health literature. Psychology is a discipline in which researchers have explored a wide range of phenomena using qualitative approaches. As with nursing, the research focus varies widely. In Rabinow (2010), bereavement of parents by children was explored using content analysis to examine interview transcripts where children described how they felt before, during, and after the loss of a parent. Butler et al. (1998) studied doctors' and patients' beliefs about the prescribing of antibiotics for sore throats, in spite of the fact that research has demonstrated that they often have no effect, while Eyler et al. (1998) used focus groups to study physical activity in minority women. Explorations of psychological and sociological phenomena such as group norms, identity, and cultural roles, can be found in the work of Syed (2010), who used narratives to study students' perceptions of ethnicity, and in the work of Nagata et al. (2010), who studied Chinese American grandmothering also by way of the narrative. Gone and Alcántara (2010) solicited stories from participants in order to examine ambitious achievement in a Native American community.

The use of qualitative approaches for data exploration is relevant across any number of disciplines and subject areas. It is easily adaptable and can be used to aid in-depth exploration of many research problems. Like the application of qualitative methods in other fields, information science and library studies can greatly benefit from its use.

References

Bowling, A. (2002) *Research Methods in Health: Investigating Health and Health Services*, 2nd edition. Buckingham, UK: Open University Press.

Brookes, D. (2007) Understanding the value of qualitative research in nursing. *Nursing Times*, 103(8), 32. Retrieved from *http://www.nursingtimes.net/nursing-practice-clinical-research/understanding-the-value-of-qualitative-research-in-nursing/201730.article*.

Butler, C.C., Rollnick, S., Pill, R., Maggs-Rapport, F. and Stott, N. (1998) Understanding the culture of prescribing: Qualitative study of general practitioners' and patients' perceptions of antibiotics for sore throats. *British Medical Journal*, 317: 637–42.

Eyler, A.A., Baker, E., Cromer, L., King, A.C., Brownson, R.C. and Donatelle, R.J. (1998) Physical activity and minority women: A qualitative study. *Health Education and Behavior*, 25: 640–52.

Georges, J.J., Grypdonck, M. and Dierckx de Casterlé, B. (2002) Being a palliative care nurse in an academic hospital: A qualitative study about nurses' perceptions of palliative care nursing. *Journal of Clinical Nursing*, 11(6): 785–93.

Gone, J.P. and Alcántara, C. (2010) The ethnographically contextualized case study method: Exploring ambitious achievement in an American Indian community. *Cultural Diversity and Ethnic Minority Psychology*, 16(2): 159–68.

Greenhalgh, T. and Taylor, R. (1997) How to read a paper: papers that go beyond numbers (qualitative research). *British Medical Journal*, 315(7110): 740–3.

Holloway, I. and Wheeler, S. (2002) *Qualitative Research in Nursing*, 2nd edition. Oxford, UK: Blackwell.

Kerr, M.P. (2002) A qualitative study of shift handover practice and function from a socio-technical perspective. *Journal of Advanced Nursing*, 37(2): 125–34.

Lefkowitz-Horowitz, H. (1988) *Campus Life: Undergraduate Cultures from the End of the Eighteenth Century to the Present*. Chicago, IL: University of Chicago Press.

McClelland, A. (1992) *The Education of Women in the United States: A Guide to Theory, Teaching, and Research*. Garland Reference Library of Social Science.

Miller Solomon, B. (1985) *In the Company of Educated Women: A History of Women and Higher Education*. New Haven, CN: Yale University Press.

Moffatt, M. (1989) *Coming of Age in New Jersey: College and American Culture*. New Brunswick, NJ: Rutgers University Press.

Munhall, P. and Oiler-Boyd, C. (eds) (1999) *Nursing Research: A Qualitative Perspective*, 3rd edition. New York: Appleton.

Nagata, D.K., Cheng, W.J.Y. and Tsai-Chae, A.H. (2010) Chinese American grandmothering: A qualitative exploration. *Asian American Journal of Psychology*, 1(2): 151–61.

Nathan, R. (2005) *My Freshman Year: What a Professor Learned by Becoming a Student*. Ithaca, NY: Cornell University Press.

Nielsen (2010) Research and measurement. Retrieved from *http://en-us.nielsen.com/content/nielsen/en_us/measurement/tv_research.html*.

Owen, D.C. (1989) Nurses' perspectives on the meaning of hope in patients with cancer: A qualitative study. *Oncology Nursing Forum*, 16(1): 75–9.

Rabinow, J. (2010) The experience of the parentally bereaved: A qualitative study. Unpublished doctoral dissertation, Graduate Studies Program in Clinical Psychology, C.W. Post, Long Island University, Brookville, New York.

Sandelowski, M. (1986) The problem of rigor in qualitative research. *Advances in Nursing Science*, 8(3): 27–37.

Sharif, F. and Masoumi, S. (2005) A qualitative study of nursing student experiences of clinical practice. *BioMed Central Nursing*, 4(6). Retrieved from *http://www.ncbi .nlm.nih.gov/pmc/articles/PMC1298307/.*

Spoelstra, S.L. and Robbins, L.B. (2010) A qualitative study of role transition from RN to APN. *International Journal of Nursing Education Scholarship*, 7(1), article 20. Retrieved from *http://www.bepress.com/ijnes/vol7/iss1/ art20/.*

Streubert, H. and Carpenter, D. (2010) *Qualitative Research in Nursing: Advancing the Humanistic Imperative.* Philadelphia, PA: Lippincott, Williams and Wilkins.

Syed, M. (2010) Memorable everyday events in college: Narratives of the intersection of ethnicity and academia. *Journal of Diversity in Higher Education*, 3(1): 56–69.

3

Ethnographic research practices in library settings

Abstract: This chapter presents information on the use of ethnographic and related approaches within library settings. Historical application of library community analysis is explored. Several recent examples are presented.

Key words: University of Rochester, Rutgers University, anthropology, ethnographic approaches, ethnography, community analysis.

Key concepts of ethnographic research

Ethnographic research is a cross-disciplinary, qualitative research approach grown out of the disciplines of anthropology and sociology, and used in a variety of other areas such as psychology (social, educational, behavioral, and organizational), business, the health sciences, and, more recently, within library, information, and computing science. It seems a particularly relevant approach for library settings, since libraries can be as complicated, diverse, and misunderstood at times as any other organization, culture, or environment.

Ethnographic research is described most simply as "an approach to learning about the social and cultural life of communities, institutions, and other settings" (Schensul et al., 1999, p. 1). One of the hallmarks of ethnographic research is the end product—an ethnography—a written account of all observations, conversations, discoveries, and insights gathered during the research process, compiled in a meaningful way. Fetterman (1998) described writing the ethnography as "the art and science of describing a group or culture" (p. 1), and the ethnographer as both "storyteller and scientist" (p. 2). Fetterman goes on to say that "the ethnographer writes about the routine, daily lives of people. The more predictable patterns of human thought and behavior are the focus of inquiry" (1998, p. 1). The goal is to observe and study as many components of the environment as possible—because the elements taken together will provide a more complete understanding than looking at any one person, small group, trend, trait, or behavior, alone. The ethnography can contain many elements. LeCompte and Schensul (1999) list the following components: beliefs, attitudes, perceptions, emotions, verbal and non-verbal means of communication; social networks, behaviors of the group of individuals with friends, family, associates, fellow workers, and colleagues; use of tools, technology, and manufacture of materials and artifacts; and patterned use of space and time (1999, p. 4).

On a practical level, ethnographic research can be a means by which researchers attempt to learn more about and contribute to solving some of society's most pressing problems (LeCompte and Schensul, 1999). Discovery is a key concept in ethnographic research, one that sets it apart from other methods of inquiry. As LeCompte and Schensul put it, "ethnography assumes that we must first discover *what* people actually do and the reasons they give for doing it" (1999, p. 2), before making any types of assumptions or interpretations. More specifically, "the tools of ethnography are designed for discovery . . . the basic tools of ethnography use the researcher's eyes and ears as the primary modes for data collection" (LeCompte and Schensul, 1992, p. 2). A second difference is the lack of control that ethnographers have over the environments that they are studying—"the ethnographic field situation is unlike clinic or laboratory-based experimental research, where most aspects of the environment are controlled and where researchers can use the same instruments and can expect to get the same results if the study is repeated" (LeCompte and Schensul, 1999, p. 2).

Ethnographic research operates with certain frameworks that influence how the method is used by researchers, depending on the researcher's own theoretical framework and the area of interest (LeCompte and Schensul, 1999, p. 41). There are five distinct paradigms that can guide ethnographic research (LeCompte and Schensul, 1999). They are the positivist paradigm, the critical paradigm, the constructivist paradigm, the ecological paradigm, and the emerging social network paradigm (1999, p. 41). In addition to these descriptions, one can also refer to a variety of ethnographic schools of thought which reference the same paradigms. The holistic variety requires that researchers spend time in the environment they are studying, and have "empathy and identification with the social grouping being observed" (Myers, 1999, p. 7). The "thick description" approach was first described by anthropologist Clifford Geertz (1973), and requires the ethnographer to "search out and analyze symbolic forms—words, images, institutions, behaviors—with respect to one another and to the whole that they comprise" (Myers, 1999, p. 8). The ethnographer does not need to immerse him- or herself deeply in the environment or culture here, as is the case with the holistic approach. Critical ethnography features a completely different approach that involves the researcher participating in an ongoing dialogue and discussion with those who are being studied, with the specific goal of surfacing "hidden agendas, power centers, and assumptions that inhibit, repress, and contain" (Thomas, 1993, p. 2).

As with all research, ethnographic research begins with a single idea, question, problem, issue, or concern that the researcher(s) want to find out more about. It can have both qualitative and quantitative elements, but the primary foundation of all ethnographic research is the act of observation. Typically, ethnographic research is done in the field, and requires that the researchers be present and immersed in the culture or environment they are studying. Conklin (1968) describes it this way:

> Ethnography involves a long period of intimate study and residence in a well-defined community employing a wide range of observational techniques including prolonged face-to-face contact with members of local groups, direct participation in some of the group's activities, and a greater emphasis on intensive work with informants than on the use of documentary or survey data. (1968, p. 172)

The participation of the ethnographer is a key element in this particular type of ethnographic work—they engage in observing what is going on around them, but they also talk to those in the community about what they observe, they look for patterns, they ask questions, and try to experience what they learn. It is in many ways the exact opposite of experimental research done in a lab—where the researcher is separated from what they are observing by a microscope lens, a cage, or a screen. The more immersed an ethnographer can become in the environment, the better the ethnography in the end. At the same time, the ethnographer must remain completely open to what they see, hear, and learn. In this way, all of the observations and important inputs become a part of the ethnography, making it more comprehensive and meaningful.

Van Maanen (1979) discusses the use of ethnographic research in the study of organizations, and sees the method as providing a way for researchers to "come to grips with the essential ethnographic question of what it is to be rather than to see a member of the organization" (p. 539). This can also be said of *being* vs. *seeing* those who are members of different cultures, groups, and institutions. This experiential component can often reveal information not obtained by other means of data collection.

LeCompte and Schensul (1999) also mention the importance of valuing the context and customs that are being studied, and refer to the "integrity of local cultures" (1999, p. 3). Simply put, ethnographic researchers are bound to respect the communities and people they come into contact with, making sure that methods for observation and data gathering are not intrusive or offensive, and that they fall within ethical guidelines.

Historically, the best-known ethnographies come out of anthropology—for instance, *The Nuer* by E.E. Evans-Pritchard (1940; first American edition 1969); *The Dynamics of Clanship Among the Tallensi* by Meyer Fortes (1945); *African Systems of Kinship and Marriage* by A.R. Radcliffe Brown and Daryll Forde (1950); *Argonauts of the Western Pacific* by Bronislaw Malinowski (1922); *Coming of Age in Samoa* by Margaret Mead (1928); and *Naven: A Survey of the Problems Suggested by a Composite Picture of the Culture of a New Guinea Tribe Drawn from Three Points of View* by Gregory Bateson (1958). Despite the fact that the better-known historical studies took place in far-away places, ethnographic research can take place and be applicable whenever there are groups and communities to be studied—from state agencies to public schools to libraries to hospitals.

Historical application within libraries and information settings

The use of ethnographic methods to investigate bibliographic trends, library services, and information systems is not a recent development. What *is* new is the increased publicity and attention that some library research projects have attracted. *Studying Students: The Undergraduate Research Project at the University of Rochester* (Foster and Gibbons, 2007) is a good example of this. This project, which began in 2004, has so far produced a book of the same title, been presented at numerous conferences, and has formed the basis of a number of instructional workshops on undergraduate and faculty research behavior sponsored by the Council on Library and Information Resources (CLIR, 2010). As early as 1896, librarians were beginning to recognize that, in order to provide better library services, they needed to be far more sensitive and informed about the community and surrounding environment. Mary Cutler (1896) talked specifically about a process that would later be referred to as community analysis—suggesting that librarians be proactive in learning about their surrounding community, in order to "catch the spirit of the civic life and relate the library to the whole" (1896, p. 448). Community analysis, an activity that involves gathering a wide variety of information about the community in order to evaluate current services and plan for the future, was seen as being an "essential element of librarianship" (Sarling and Van Tassel, 1999, p. 7). A number of authors have written about the application of the community analysis within libraries, including Bone (1976), Wheeler (1924), and Carnovosky and Martin (1944).

Although community analysis is not classified as a type of qualitative or interpretive research, nor designed to produce an ethnography, the elements and activities needed to assemble the analysis have much in common with the ethnographic approach. Paying attention to everyday details in all areas of the community and formulating a sense of not just who the members are, but also context and meaning, are critical. Evans (1976) suggests that the community analysis "is as basic to library management as the physician's diagnosis is to the practice of medicine" (1976, p. 454). Greer and Hale (1982) are well-known for developing the Community Analysis Research Institute (CARI) model, which provides an actual format for community analysis. The model provides a way to systematically collect, organize, and analyze data about the library, its users, and the community (Greer and Hale, 1982, p. 358). Sarling and Van Tassel (1999) provide this comprehensive overview of the CARI model:

> The Community Analysis Research Institute (CARI) model begins with a focus on the community from four perspectives—individuals, groups, agencies and lifestyles—and incorporates both quantitative and qualitative research methods to collect a variety of data including demographic characteristics, history of the community, topographical features, transportation routes and traffic patterns, commercial activities, communication patterns, housing, education, cultural activities, health facilities, employment, recreation entertainment, and the characteristic lifestyles of the community and its sub-cultures. (1999, pp. 8, 9)

In Grace Stingly's 1919 "Studying a Community in Order to Render Better Library Service," Stingly detailed an ethnographic approach to learning more about the environment to improve the library's outreach and services, and described areas for data collection and observation that closely match those described in the CARI model some 63 years later. She states, "to serve a community efficiently the librarian must know that community physically, mentally, and morally. She must know the kind of people with which she deals, the things in which they are interested, their industries, their schools, their churches, their amusements, their health conditions, their public press, their government. To do this the community must be studied" (Stingly, 1919, p. 157). Stingly then cites 18 different areas for study and observation, essentially outlining at least some of the components that one might find in an ethnography of any community:

1. *Physical aspects of the city*—Including status of roads and infrastructure, presence of any federal buildings, municipal or private utilities, presence of parks, presence of natural attractions such as lakes.

2. *Civic organizations*—Presence of civic or public improvement agencies.

3. *Historical background of the city*—Date city was founded and under what conditions, most important factors in the city's industrial, social and political growth.

4. *Population*—Total population, percentage of foreign inhabitants, geographical distribution of the population, location of various district types (urban, suburban, working class, middle class, etc.), per cent of the total population served by the library, library's reach into all segments of the population.

5. *Immigrants*—Including such indicators as literacy, primary industries for employment, attendance of English classes, geographical distribution for immigrant residents, participation in political process.

6. *Industry*—Businesses and manufacturers located in the city, percentage of the population employed in factories, presence of vocational training, library presence in factories and manufacturing plants (via signage, special programs, etc.), library collections relevant to local business and commerce.

7. *Health*—Presence of a board of health, publication of important health reports and communications, presence of private researchers or others who study health-related concerns, presence of disease and illness prevention educational campaigns, presence of a hospital, presence of a visiting nurse service.

8. *Child Welfare*—Presence of child welfare and related agencies, provision of materials related to child welfare, participation by local medical professionals in prevention and educational programs.

9. *Charity*—Presence of charitable organizations, cooperation of these organizations with the library for educational purposes.

10. *Schools*—Number of public schools in the area, how close the schools are to a library, presence of libraries in the schools and their condition, number of teachers in the community, public library presence in the schools through special programs, bookmobile and librarian visits, presence of vocational, parochial and private schools, presence of college, university or special libraries in the area, use of public libraries by college and university students for research.

11. *Churches*—Number of churches in the city, use of the libraries by Sunday school teachers and missionary societies, use of the libraries by ministers and other members of the clergy, use of the libraries by young people's religious groups.

12. *Clubs*—Presence of women's clubs, use of clubs by the library, presence of Boy Scouts, Girl Scouts and use of the library.

13. *Newspapers*—Number of newspapers published in the area, publication languages, editorial stance towards the library.

14. *Book stores*—Opportunities for private buyers, number of bookstores in the area, quality of children's books selection.

15. *Recreation*—Presence of theater, little league, drama club, amusement parks, movie theaters, and playgrounds; library story hours at local playgrounds, local celebrations including parades and festivals, library participation in local celebrations.

16. *Municipal government*—Size of the city council, how well city council members know the library, attitude of the mayor towards the library, budget and fiscal management processes, library provision of reading materials to jails, police and fire stations.

17. *Situation of the library*—Where the library is located and impact on use.

18. *Extension work*—Impact of the library on areas outside of the local geographic boundaries.

(Stingly, 1919, pp. 158–61)

While information in each of these areas might be gathered via surveys and questionnaires, the ideal method would be active observation, over a period of time, as well as participation by the librarians on some level to provide a sense of context and meaning. The interaction of residents with each of these structures and the impacts on their lives would reveal the richest data.

The library is but one small component of today's information environment, and the average user/consumer probably prefers more immediate access to information via the Internet. Another reason that ethnographic approaches might be even more relevant today is the growing disparate nature of information users. It is becoming increasingly difficult to categorize users and forecast the types of services, resources, and information systems they might need now and in the future; even more recent trends for predicting and categorizing user interaction behavior, such as the use of personas in interface design (Dantin, 2005) are fading. Evans (1976) alluded to this as well when he explained the usefulness of the community analysis when trying to provide services for a complex community (1976, p. 443).

Another concept rarely mentioned in the library or information science research literature, but closely related to ethnographic research, is that of naturalistic inquiry. Mellon (1986) writes, "research in library science has, for many years, meant quantitative research, an objective method of study which seeks facts and causes generalizable from one situation to another" (p. 349). "While much has been learned using these methods, the fact remains that not all questions in library science can be quantified" (p. 349). The author goes on to suggest that librarians "explore the flexibility and humanist perspective of naturalistic inquiry" (p. 349). The inherent philosophical differences between naturalistic inquiry and quantitative inquiry often lead to misunderstandings about the validity of naturalistic studies (p. 349), but Mellon cautions that these disagreements are actually born out of not understanding the naturalistic approach. Mellon (1986) clarifies the goal of naturalistic inquiry, to provide "in-depth, descriptive answers" (p. 349) to the question of social phenomenon characteristics, with the aim of "understanding the phenomenon rather than controlling it" (p. 350).

Klopfer (2004) also addresses the role of ethnography in library research, and stresses the importance of looking at the library within the context of the community, stating that "library studies would benefit from broader ethnographic research that places libraries in communities and societies" (2004, p. 106). Klopfer defines library-related ethnography as "an approach that takes into account the holistic, systematic nature of institutions, and one that explores meaning within a social structure. Locating meaning within a special structure is particularly important in order to avoid the risk of a vaguely "cultural" study that, having no context, easily falls into essentialist, teleological pseudo-explanations along the lines of 'they do it because it is their culture'" (Klopfer, 2004, p. 106).

Examples of recent ethnographic research in library environments

There has been a recent growing interest in ethnographic research within information environments such as libraries. Much of the literature presents research done in academic library settings, but there is also similar work being done in other types of library environments (see the Rural Uganda Library study below). This interest crosses disciplinary boundaries; for instance, the 2009 American Anthropological Association 108th Annual Meeting had as one of its themes "Practicing Anthropology in the Shelves: Designing Academic Libraries via Ethnography," with several high-profile presenters and a number of presentations from libraries currently involved in their own ethnographic projects. A few examples of some recent applications of the ethnographic approach are listed below. It should be noted that although many of these projects utilize methods of observation, data collection, analysis, and documentation that are commonly used within ethnographic fieldwork, not all produce an actual ethnography at the project's end.

Preschoolers' use of public libraries

In 1996, McKechnie conducted a study of 30 preschool girls in order to document their public library use. The author reveals that one of the main reasons for using an ethnographic approach had to do with the audience: "Because of their dependence on language and interpersonal relationships, interviews are not suitable for use with preschoolers. Similarly, as very young children are unable to read, written questionnaires are of no use for data collection either" (2000, p. 62). The study used three different means of data collection: audiorecording of children's naturally occurring talk, participant observation, and diary keeping by key informants/ observers (McKechnie, 2000, p. 62). The study generated more than 2,000 pages of data, and the author states that "analysis of the data allowed me to construct a detailed, rich picture of what preschool girls actually do while at the library and while using library materials at home as well as to identify some of the impacts, including learning opportunities, provided by library services and collections" (2000, p. 72).

Anthropologist in the library: helping librarians support student success

This study, which began in 2009, received a large grant to hire an anthropologist to design and conduct an ethnographic study of how students at Illinois Wesleyan University work, with a specific emphasis on how they use the library. A diverse team utilized photo journals, ethnographic videos, mapping exercises, and interviews to collect data. The project is expected to take two years to complete, and the results are to be used to help improve library outreach and services (Anthropology and the Ames Library, 2009).

California State University Fresno Henry Madden Library ethnographic study

This research also sought to investigate the use and meaning of the library to students on its campus. Student behavior and conceptions of things like "reference" and "library resources" were studied. A variety of methods were used including observation, interviews, and photo journaling (American Anthropological Association, 2009).

The MIT student photo diary study

This 2006 study used photographs to document students' information-seeking behaviors, and followed ethnographic guidelines for their analysis. The aim of the study was to use found information about research behaviors in order to design the library's information services and systems to be more supportive of research needs. The project "generated 275 distinct information-seeking tasks used by students" (Gabridge, Gaskell and Stout, 2008).

The University of Rochester Libraries study of undergraduates

This is perhaps the most widely known academic library-related ethnographic study to date, and certainly the study that provided the framework for the other academic library ethnographic studies mentioned in this list. Foster and Gibbons (2007) explained the impetus for the study in the introduction to the book *Studying Students: The Undergraduate Research Project at the University of Rochester*: "The library staff wanted to do more to reach students and their instructors in support of the university's educational mission. But to do more we realized we needed to know more about today's undergraduate students—their habits, the academic work they are required to do, and their library-related needs. In particular, we were interested in how students write their research papers and what services, resources, and facilities would be most useful to them" (Foster and Gibbons, 2007, p. v). The project had as one of its hallmarks the participation of an integrated team of librarians, IT specialists, designers, and an anthropologist to lead the study. The researchers spent time in student dormitories, changed reference hours to be more in line with student hours (i.e., very, very late nights), had students document their own living and studying environments by taking Polaroid photos, interviewed faculty about their expectations of students, conducted impromptu interviews with and surveys of students outside of the library, and created tracking/mapping diaries of the physical places where students spent their time. The immersion of the researchers in the lives of the students was a key element in this study. To date, a monograph, many workshops and presentations have resulted from the study.

Rutgers University Libraries student behaviors and website redesign study

Modeled after the Rochester study, the Rutgers study (Rutgers University Libraries, 2009) used an ethnographic approach to redesign the library's website. An anthropologist was hired to lead a mixed team of librarians, students, systems staff, and administrators through the process of designing and implementing an ethnographic study. The study focused on how graduates, undergraduates, and faculty used the library website, and, more importantly, how their research habits influence their work and the use of the library's resources. The study and resulting design work are still underway. More about the Rutgers study can be found in Chapters 6 and 9.

Uganda rural village library study

This longitudinal study is an example of library-based ethnographic field research set in a remote, developing area of the world. Researchers have been studying the impact of rural village libraries on the lives of villagers in rural Uganda since 2004 (Dent and Yannotta, 2005; Dent, 2006a, 2006b, 2007). The work includes extended stays in the village, and participation in the lives of the residents on a variety of levels. The study is a more typical model of traditional ethnographic field research. More about the Uganda study can be found in Chapter 8.

Ethnographic research in information systems design and evaluation

The use of ethnographic and other similar qualitative research approaches for information systems research is not new, but is not often used. Myers (1999) suggests that "ethnographic research is well suited to providing information systems researchers with rich insights into the human, social, and organizational aspects of information systems" (1999, p. 2).

Myers also suggests that the transformation of information systems and the growing focus on the end user's social, behavioral, and organizational contexts make the ethnographic approach most appropriate (1999, p. 4). Walsham (1995) refers to the emergence of ethnographic research as "an important strand in information systems research" (p. 75). Harvey and Myers (1995) add: "Because ethnography deals with actual practices in real world situations, it allows for relevant issues to be explored and frameworks to be developed which can be used by both practitioners and researchers" (1995, p. 18).

More broadly, some scholars advocate for the "role of anthropology as a source discipline for information systems" (Avison and Myers, 1995, p. 43), highlighting the inherent connection between information technology and organizational culture. Olson (1982) and Schein (1984) are perhaps two of the better-known scholars to explicate this relationship. How users of technology make sense of the world around them, their cultures, their organizations, and the extent to which information technology plays a role in this sense-making is clearly akin to anthropological studies of culture, meaning, and symbolism.

Ethnographic research for information systems has been discussed in the literature by a number of researchers (Prasad, 1997; Harvey, 1997; Suchman, 1987; Myers, 1997; Pettigrew, 1985; Preston, 1991; Davies, 1991; Randall et al., 1999; Wynn, 1991; Lee, 1991; Harvey and Myers, 1995). Orlikowski (1991) studied a large software company, where she spent eight months immersing herself in the culture. Her ethnography is frequently referenced in the information systems literature when referring to ethnographic research application. In the early 1990s, researchers in the United Kingdom used an ethnographic approach to study the habits of air traffic controllers, with the end goal of informing the design of an air traffic control information system (Bentley et al., 1992). The researchers reveal how ethnographic studies helped them "gain an understanding of the cooperative processes of air traffic control and how this understanding has influenced the design of our prototype software system" (1992, p. 124). "During this study, software engineers, an ethnographer, a sociologist, and air traffic controllers worked collaboratively to identify the various elements of teamwork critical to air traffic control, including the type of conversations and talk around the suite, the type of activities performed, and "the stories and anecdotes told" (1992, p. 126). Most importantly, the researchers discuss how the ethnographic approach helped to challenge some widely held but inaccurate beliefs about air traffic controller behavior, which in turn had a positive impact on the systems design.

More recently, Hartmann et al. (2009) described several information system architecture, engineering, and construction projects that utilized ethnographic methods to inform the development of these systems. The authors provide an in-depth overview of an "ethnographic-action research cycle for the development of an information system" (2009, p. 57). They credit the iterative nature of this process with helping developers to create a more robust and responsive system (2009, p. 66).

What makes the findings from these projects so different from those revealed via non-ethnographic approaches? The data gathered for each of these projects are unique in that they are the result of observation done in natural, real-life settings. Typically, these very rich data reveal insights, a way to see inside, that are not "visible" via conventional methods. An example of a finding from the Rochester study illustrates this point perfectly. Librarians asked students to take pictures that were representative of their lives as students.

Below is the description of one of their most interesting revelations.

> In one instance, it was the absence of something that caught our attention. In photographs showing "all the stuff you take to class," we observed that laptops were not included, even though students had laptops. So, we noted it down without understanding why, until the mapping diaries, with more data about students' days, provided an answer. That is when we discovered how itinerant students were during the day, carrying what they needed for long stretches. They covered a lot of territory, and it simply was not practical for most to include a laptop along with all the other things they brought to classes. Instead, laptops came out when students planned to be in one place for a while to do their work, such as in the library at night. (Foster and Gibbons, 2007, pp. 46, 47)

The researchers stressed that these photo surveys and diaries allowed students to share "details about their lives in a way that conventional interviews alone could not achieve" (Foster and Gibbons, 2007, p. 47).

In the ethnographic research project to inform the design of an air traffic control system (Bentley et al., 1992), researchers also found that this type of approach produced novel findings: "Our ethnographic observations revealed that the manual manipulation of flight strips and the manual re-ordering of the flight strip racks were significant activities" (1992, p. 128). As a result, the design prototype incorporated a number of decisions which reflected this discovery.

McKechnie (2000) also highlights findings that were exclusive to the ethnographic orientation of the research. Girls' use of public libraries was framed primarily by the continued use of library materials at home, the sharing of these materials with other family members, and the reading of these materials over and over (McKechnie, 2000). All of these observations were made and recorded by the mothers of the young girls in diaries provided as part of the study. Again, this is not the type of information and subsequent finding that could be easily gleaned from a survey or even from an interview.

Balancing quantitative and qualitative approaches to library research

In many library settings, research is often conducted by the gathering of quantitative data that are later interpreted by library staff and translated into action items—changes and improvements to services, collections, and facilities that can be acted upon. Increasingly, library users are in search of better user experiences—improvements that cannot be communicated via survey or statistical data. As Mellon (1986) suggests, not all answers within the library environment are quantifiable. Typical approaches to data gathering within library environments are surveys, both home-grown and commercial products such as *LibQual*, door counts, print circulation statistics, and electronic resource use statistics. Surveys are particularly popular—as of 2007, the *LibQual* survey has been given to approximately a million library users (*LibQual*, 2009) at more than a thousand libraries. *LibQual* features both quantitative feedback and open-ended questions, which yield qualitative data. However, librarians readily share that even surveys such as this fall short when it comes to providing a comprehensive and true understanding of user needs in relation to library service and quality.

Is it really possible to have both a conceptual and practical understanding of user needs, and to then translate those ideas into tangible service improvements? Integrating quantitative approaches such as surveys and statistical data gathering with observational approaches such as those common in ethnographic research may yield interesting and useful results. Librarians and others interested in research to improve library and information services may want to consider a survey first, to highlight areas for further investigation, followed by targeted field studies. These field studies might include observation of users, impromptu discussions with users about their work and use of the library, focus groups, more formal interviews with users, and the collection of user "artifacts" such as photographs of where users work, where they travel on campus (for academic libraries), and their research "diaries." Each of these methods has been used in the examples of ethnographic library projects mentioned earlier in this chapter. Not only are these methods sometimes the perfect research complement to quantitative data; they are often far more engaging and stimulating, and yield much richer data than survey answers or figures alone.

Users tend to find ways to create better experiences for themselves; thus, consistent observation is a very important component for those working in libraries. What types of "workarounds" do users come up with when something does not work? Where do different groups of users tend to congregate in the library? Do users tend to move the furniture in the library around, no matter how many times librarians put it back? How many times on average does a user leave his or her seat in the library, and why? Are there certain areas in the public library where parents feel more comfortable letting young children explore? Are there areas where the children appear to be more relaxed and ready to read?

These behaviors are best observed, and sometimes the best ideas for great change can come from these simple observations.

Implications and challenges

Van Maanen (1979) writes: "Ethnographic research is guided as much by drift as design and is perhaps the source of far more failures than successes. Assuming an ethnographic stance is by no means a guarantee that one will collect accurate and theoretically useful data no matter how long one remains in the field" (p. 539).

Conducting any type of methodological research within a busy library or information setting can be a challenge. For many organizations, in-depth research of this type is just not possible. Another real challenge is the appropriate selection and application of ethnographic methods, which can easily be confused with other similar approaches such as ethnomethodology. The greatest part of research done in libraries and information settings is trying to address some problem, or improvement, on behalf of the user. Thus, it is important for information service organizations to evaluate the appropriateness of an ethnographic approach for their environment before embarking on related studies. Klein and Myers (1999) provide guidelines for the use of qualitative methods in the area of information systems evaluation that might be relevant for other information settings as well. The authors ask several questions. Is the output—the ethnography—a contribution to the field? Does the author offer rich insights? Has a significant amount of material been collected? Is there sufficient information about the research methods being used? (Myers, 1999, pp. 11, 12).

In perhaps the most rigorous discussion of the use and misuse of ethnographic research methods in library and information science (LIS) research is the *Library Quarterly* article by Sandstrom and Sandstrom (1995). The article challenges the sometimes misguided application of anthropologic methods within LIS research, and offers some suggestions for staying true to the form. The authors state: "Various disciplines and professional fields along with LIS have moved to embrace qualitative and field-observational methods, including communications, biomedical informatics, educational research, organizational research and political science" (Sandstrom and Sandstrom, 1995, p. 162). They go on to add that, "unfortunately, the antiscientific values that underlie much of LIS writing on the subject promise to rob qualitative methods of their considerate power to elucidate social processes" (1995, p. 162). The failure of the profession to apply ethnographic methods with the appropriate consideration of both philosophical and scientific inquiry frameworks is summarized by the authors as five distinct issues: scientific versus nonscientific traditions; the distinction between emic and etic perspectives; the artificial divide between qualitative and quantitative techniques; inductive vs. deductive research strategies; and the challenges of portraying real people with scientific reports (Sandstrom and Sandstrom, 1995, p. 161). These tensions have not been addressed or resolved within information science, according to the authors, who caution, "Unfortunately, when methods and conceptual frameworks are translated from one discipline to another, their rationale is sometimes lost in the process. This loss of rationale has clearly been the case when LIS researchers have adopted qualitative, and, in particular, ethnographic methods. It is interesting that in the growing body of LIS scholarship dealing with qualitative research practice, publications on methodology written by anthropologists are rarely cited"

(Sandstrom and Sandstrom, 1995, p. 163). The article goes on to suggest a variety of solutions to these challenges.

This article was written in 1995, and a quick scan of more current LIS literature does indeed feature references to some anthropological literature (Klein and Myers, 1999; Avison and Myers, 1995; McKechnie, 2000), so perhaps the profession is becoming more mindful of incorporating not just stand-alone methods, but recognizing the importance of disciplinary foundations as well.

The ethnographic approach can be a most rewarding experience, and one that provides data not able to be gathered by any other means. It also comes with a number of considerations that must be evaluated before any action is taken, including, as Sandstrom and Sandstrom (1995) suggest, a more rigorous alignment with the scientific foundations of the method. For those who are interested in investigating new methods for conducting research with the end goal of improving information systems, user services, outreach, and user experience, it may certainly be worth a further look.

References

American Anthropological Association (2009) *Practicing anthropology in the shelves: Designing academic libraries via ethnography.* 108th Annual Meeting of the AAA Retrieved from *http://theanthroguys.com/2009/08/05/ practicing-anthropology-in-the-shelves-designing-academic-libraries-via-ethnography/.*

Anthropology and the Ames Library (2009) *A study of how students study.* Retrieved from *http://www.iwu.edu/ CurrentNews/newsreleases09/news_AmesLSTAGrant 00509.shtml.*

Avison, D. and Myers, M. (1995) Information systems and anthropology: An anthropological perspective on IT and organizational culture. *Information Technology and People*, 8(3): 43–53.

Bateson, G. (1958) *Naven: A Survey of the Problems Suggested by a Composite Picture of the Culture of a New Guinea Tribe Drawn from Three Points of View*. Stanford, CA: Stanford University Press.

Bentley, R., Hughes, J.A., Randall, D., Rodden, T., Sawyer, P., Shapiro, D. and Sommerville, I. (1992) Ethnographically informed systems design for air traffic control. In *Proceedings of the ACM Conference on Computer Supported Cooperative Work*, 123–9. New York: ACM.

Bone, L. (1976) Library trends: Community analysis and libraries. *Library Trends*, 24(3): 429–619.

Carnovosky, L. and Martin, L. (1944) *The Library in the Community*. Chicago, IL: University of Chicago Press.

Conklin, H. (1968) Ethnography. In D.L. Sills (ed.), *International Encyclopedia of the Social Sciences* (pp. 115–208). New York: Free Press.

Council on Library and Information Resources (CLIR) (2010) Faculty research behavior workshops. Retrieved from *http://www.clir.org/activities/details/faculty.html*.

Cutler, M. (1896) Two fundamentals. *Library Journal*, 21: 446–9.

Dantin, U. (2005) Application of personas in user interface design for educational software. In *Proceedings of the Seventh Australasian Computing Education Conference*, 239–47. Newcastle, Australia.

Davies, L. (1991) Researching the organizational culture contexts of information systems strategy. In H.E. Nissen, H.K. Klein, and R.A. Hirscheim (eds) *Information systems research: Contemporary approaches and emergent traditions*. Amsterdam: North Holland.

Dent, V. (2006a) Modelling the rural community library: Characteristics of the Kitengesa Library in rural Uganda. *New Library World*, 107(1/2): 16–30.

Dent, V. (2006b) Observations of school library impact at two rural Ugandan schools. *New Library World*, 107(9/10): 403–21.

Dent, V. (2007) Local economic development in Uganda and the connection to rural community libraries and literacy. *New Library World*, 108 (5/6): 203–17.

Dent, V. and Yannotta, L. (2005) A rural community library in Uganda: A study of its use and users. *Libri International Journal of Libraries and Information Services*, 55(1): 39–55.

Evans, C. (1976) A history of community analysis in American librarianship. *Library Trends*, 24(3): 441–57.

Evans-Pritchard, E.E. (1969) *The Nuer: A Description of the Modes of Livelihood and Political Institutions of a Nilotic People*. London: Oxford University Press.

Fetterman, D.M. (1998) *Ethnography: Step by step*, 2nd edition. Newbury Park, CA: Sage Publications.

Fortes, M. (1945) *The dynamics of clanship among the Tallensi; Being the first part of an analysis of the social structure of a Trans-Volta tribe*. London: Oxford University Press.

Foster, N. and Gibbons, S. (2007) Studying students: The undergraduate research project at the University of Rochester. Retrieved from *http://hdl.handle.net/1802/7520*.

Gabridge, T., Gaskell, M. and Stout, A. (2008) Information seeking through students' eyes: The MIT photo diary study. *College and Research Libraries*, 69(6): 510–22.

Geertz, C. (1973) Thick description: Toward an interpretive theory of culture. In *The Interpretation of Cultures: Selected Essays*. New York: Basic Books.

Greer, R. and Hale, M. (1982) The community analysis process. In J. Robbins-Carter (ed.), *Public Librarianship: A Reader* (pp. 358–67). Englewood, CO: Libraries Unlimited.

Hartmann, T., Fischer, M. and Haymaker, J. (2009) Implementing information systems with project teams using ethnographic-action research. *Advanced Engineering Informatics*, 23(1): 57–67.

Harvey, L. (1997) A discourse on ethnography. In A.S. Lee, J. Liebenau, and J.I. DeGross (eds), *Information Systems and Qualitative Research* (pp. 207–224). London: Chapman and Hall.

Harvey, L. and Myers, M. (1995) Scholarship and practice: The contribution of ethnographic research methods to bridging the gap. *Information Technology and People*, 8(3): 13–27.

Klein, H. and Myers, M. (1999) A set of principles for conducting and evaluating interpretive field studies in information systems. *MIS Quarterly*, 23(1): 67–93.

Klopfer, L. (2004) Commercial libraries in an Indian city: An ethnographic sketch. *Libri*, 54: 104–12.

LeCompte, M. and Schensul, J. (1999) *Designing and Conducting Ethnographic Research*. Walnut Creek, CA: Altamira Press.

Lee, A. (1991) Integrating positivist and interpretive approaches to organizational research. *Organization Science*, 2(4): 342–65.

LibQual (2009) Retrieved from *http://www.libqual.org/home*.

Malinowski, B. (1922) *Argonauts of the Western Pacific. An account of native enterprise and adventure in the archipelagoes of Melanesian New Guinea*. London: George Routledge.

McKechnie, L. (2000) Ethnographic observation of pre-school children. *Library and Information Science Research*, 22(1): 61–76.

Meade, M. (1928) *Coming of Age in Samoa. A psychological study of primitive youth for Western Civilization.* V. Morrow. London, United Kingdom.

Mellon, C. (1986) Understanding library use from the standpoint of the user: Naturalistic inquiry for library research. *Journal of Educational Media and Library Sciences*, 23(4): 348–64.

Myers, M. (1999) Investigating information systems with ethnographic research. *Communications of the AIS*, 2(23): 2–19.

Myers, M. (1997) Critical ethnography in information systems. In A.S. Lee, J. Liebenau, and J.I. DeGross (eds), *Information systems and qualitative research* (pp. 276–300). London: Chapman and Hall.

Olson, M. (1982) New information technology and organizational culture. *MIS Quarterly*, 6(5): 71–92.

Orlikowski, W. (1991) Integrated information environment or matrix of control? The contradictory implications of information technology. *Accounting, Management and Information Technologies*, 1(1): 9–42.

Pettigrew, A. (1985) Contextualist research and the study of organizational change processes. In E. Mumford, R. Hirschheim, G. Fitzgerald, and A.T. Wood-Harper (eds), *Research methods in information systems*. New York: North Holland.

Prasad, P. (1997) Systems of meaning: Ethnography as a methodology for the study of information technologies. In A.S. Lee, J. Liebenau, and J.I. DeGross (eds), *Information Systems and Qualitative Research* (pp. 101–18). London: Chapman and Hall.

Preston, A. (1991) The problem in and of management information systems. *Accounting, Management and Information Technologies*, 1(1): 43–69.

Radcliffe Brown, A.R. and Forde, D. (1950) *African Systems of Kinship and Marriage*. London: Oxford University Press.

Randall, D., Hughes, J.A., O'Brien, J., Rodden, T., Rouncefield, M., Sommerville, I., and Tolmie, P. (1999) Banking on the old technology: Understanding the organizational context of legacy issues. *Communications of the AIS*, 2(8): 1–27.

Rutgers University Libraries (2009) Library ethnographic project underway. Retrieved from *http://rulerp.blogspot.com/2009/03/getting-started-rul-ethnographic-web.html*.

Sandstrom, A. and Sandstrom, P. (1995) The use and misuse of anthropological methods in library and information science research. *Library Quarterly*, 65(2): 161–99.

Sarling, H. and Van Tassel, D. (1999) Community analysis: Research that matters to a north-central Denver community. *Library and Information Science Research*, 21(1): 7–29.

Schein, E.H. (1984) Coming to a new awareness of organizational culture. *Sloan Management Review*, 25: 3–16.

Schensul, S., Schensul, J. and LeCompte, M. (1999) *Essential Ethnographic Methods*. Walnut Creek, CA: Altamira Press.

Stingly, G. (1919) Studying a community in order to render better library service. *Library Occurrent*, 5: 156–62.

Suchman, L. (1987) *Plans and Situated Actions: The Problem of Human-machine Communication*. Cambridge, MA: Cambridge University Press.

Thomas, J. (1993) *Doing Critical Ethnography*. Newbury Park, CA: Sage Publications.

Van Maanen, J. (1979) The fact of fiction in organizational ethnography. *Administrative Science Quarterly*, 24(4): 539–50.

Walsham, G. (1995) Interpretive case studies in IS research: Nature and method. *European Journal of Information Systems*, 4(2): 74–81.

Wheeler, J. (1924) *The Library and the Community*. Chicago, IL: American Library Association Publications.

Wynn, E. (1991) Taking practice seriously. In J. Greenbaum and M. Kyng (eds), *Design at work*. New Jersey: Lawrence Erlbaum.

4

Eyes wide open: using trends, professional literature, and users to create a research canvas in libraries

Abstract: This chapter explores the ways in which librarians and others might use the current literature and other professional resources to help define a research focus and better understand users. Trends in technology as possible areas for discovery are discussed.

Key words: born digital, academic libraries, cloud computing, mobile devices.

Developing a "research agenda" is often an uphill battle for libraries. It can be a difficult task, especially if the agenda is completely unattached to documented user needs and service developments. A research agenda in and of itself is virtually useless—it is time-consuming, can yield a lot of data but very little information that is actually translated into meaningful improvements for users. In the best-case scenario, research can "collaboratively identify problems and opportunities, prototype and test solutions, and share findings through publications, presentations and professional interactions" (OCLC, 2010). In any library setting, deciding on a path of research often involves other entities and considerations. On the academic campus, it would be foolish to embark on a research agenda without first being very familiar with the campus's research agenda, and without trying to create as much campus synchronicity as possible. In a public library setting, a library board or community board might be interested in certain topics, which should be considered as possible areas for further inquiry. In a research library, any research project should complement and support scholarly work currently going on in the major disciplines.

Ideally, library-related research should somehow be connected to user need. This may mean research that focuses on environmental and behavioral aspects of the user experience. In addition to being closely attuned to the changes being experienced by users both inside and outside of libraries, librarians and others who are interested in creating the best possible environments and services for users should also stay abreast of recent literature, reports, and research efforts by organizations that specialize in such. A few examples are the Council on Library and Information Resources (CLIR); the Coalition for Networked Information (CNI); the Online Computer Library Center (OCLC); the Joint Information Systems Committee (JISC); the Association of College and Research Libraries (ACRL); the American Library Association (ALA); the International Federation of Library Associations and Institutions (IFLA); the American Library Association's Library and Information Technology Association (LITA); the Research Information Network (RIN); Research Libraries UK (RLUK); the Society of College, National and University Libraries (SCONUL); the Centre for Information Behaviour and the Evaluation of Research (CIBER); "fact tanks" such as the Pew Research Center, and research organizations such as the Andrew W. Mellon Foundation, the Bill and Melinda Gates Foundation, and the Carnegie Foundation for the Advancement of Teaching.

Oftentimes, in library environments, the decision to conduct research is driven by crises, whether budgetary, staffing, or other. Research conducted in these conditions can often feel overwhelmingly critical, narrowly focused, rushed, and reactionary. It is rare to find day-to-day decisions driven by empirical research. Moreover, it is rare to find library environments where research is the norm. And rightfully so—libraries of all types are traditionally known as service environments, spaces where access to subject expertise and collections are made available to users. They are not necessarily known as places where decisions are based on research data, as is the case with profit-driven organizations.

This has been the case historically. The modern-day reality is a little different. Libraries the world over are facing the challenge of implementing drastic changes or running the risk of becoming less useful to a community of users who have unprecedented access to resources and information. There is a sense of competition, and many libraries in the West have begun to define themselves not in relation simply to their print collections, but with regard to the expertise of librarians, special collections, archives, and community programming. The Queensborough Public Library in Queens, New York, is probably best known not for its vast collection of print materials, but for the development of its "New Americans" program, which featured aggressive outreach efforts, diverse programming, and multilanguage print materials for new Americans across the borough of Queens. This program became a model for other public library systems in the United States seeking to provide more inclusive programming for an increasingly multiethnic user body. The decision to develop this type of program at the Queensborough Public Library was driven by demographic data, which suggested new Americans were increasingly moving into the borough, and were in need of a wide variety of educational and employment services (Pyati, 2003). Research into these environmental changes guided the subsequent development of the program.

Getting started is the hardest part, and in addition to being familiar with what is being talked about within the profession, and by users, a thorough literature review on the topic of interest, or on methods for investigating certain topics can also be enlightening. It is likely that someone somewhere has already investigated and written about at least some elements of any particular research topic, so a literature review can help librarians and researchers decide what *not* to research. Radford and Snelson (2009) define five current trends for library research: reference services, information literacy, collection management, knowledge organization, and leadership. Information seeking is another area that researchers continue to examine (Nicholas et al., 2009; Timmers and Glas, 2010; Jamali and Nicholas, 2010; Prendiville et al., 2009). Wildemuth (2002) provides an overview of methods to investigate information-seeking behavior, including the use of diaries, card sorts, structured observation, and ethnographies. All of these topics are relatively traditional and predictable areas for library research, but certainly still relevant. However, it is not impossible to imagine that, in the future, these areas will become less relevant, and other research areas more so, simply because of the ever-changing nature of the user and the world around us.

The trick to discovering the areas that might benefit from further exploration within any library is to find the intersection of current trends, future trends, new technologies, *and* the libraries' strategic plan, user need, and future goals. It will not always be the case that areas overlap, but there may be some commonalities that draw your attention. Using ideas generated by researching the literature, paying attention to what is happening in the surrounding world, educational trends, technology, and consumer practices, can all inform research practices. It is important that librarians be able to see the potential for these overlapping spaces in relation to what they do.

Although not all of the research material generated by research or scholarly organizations will be relevant for all libraries, there is often quite a bit of useful information that can inform research practices at the local level. The next section of this chapter will present examples of trends, changes, and developments in the library world, drawn from the literature, with a specific focus on academic and research libraries. No one type of research approach is suggested here, as you will see; these research questions may be investigated with either qualitative or quantitative methods, or both.

Generational differences and the digital landscape

There is quite a bit of literature that addresses the technological habits and behaviors of the population of people born between roughly 1980 and 1994 (Long, 2005; Oblinger, 2003; Oblinger and Oblinger, 2005; Prensky, 2001, 2005; Tapscott, 1998, 2008; Frand, 2000; Bennett et al., 2008; Jukes et al., 2010; Rosen, 2010). Prensky (2001) described this group as digital natives, Tapscott (1998) and Carlson (2005) referred to them as the "Net generation," and Howe and Strauss (2003) called them "millennials." The "Nintendo Generation" was coined by Green et al. (2003); "Cyberkids" by Facer and Furlong (2001); and "Screenagers" by Rushkoff (1996). Obviously, young people born between 1980 and 1994 are an incredibly diverse and heterogeneous group, and the global use of the terms above without differentiation has been criticized by a number of scholars (Bennett et al., 2008; Helsper, 2008). Regardless, an entirely new area of research was created around the excitement spurned by this intriguing new generation.

Juxtaposed against this new population, everyone else is digital immigrants (Prensky, 2001). Born before 1980, the group of digital immigrants "includes most teachers," who "lack the technological fluency of the digital natives and find the skills possessed by them almost completely foreign" (Bennett et al., 2008, p. 777). Digital immigrants were not born into the digital era that we find ourselves in now; they are transplants from an earlier time not defined by technology. This gap presents certain challenges, especially when it comes to teaching and education (Rosen, 2010; Jukes et al., 2010; Brown, 2002; Levin and Arafeh, 2002; Levin et al., 2002; Prensky, 2005).

According to Palfrey and Gasser (2008) "digital natives live much of their lives online, without distinguishing between the online and the offline" (p. 4). Their identities, the authors suggest, are not split into separate real and virtual identities; rather, they just have one that is a mixture of both online and offline representations (p. 4). Palfrey and Gasser (2008) present a mixture of anecdotal and demographic data to support their idea of what it means to be born digital. One of the more critical observations in terms of libraries and other information spaces is how digital natives relate to information, which is drastically different from the way their parents relate to information. "Digital natives are coming to rely upon this connected space for virtually all of the information they need to live their lives" (p. 6). "They have little use for those big maps you have to fold on the creases, or for TV listings, travel guides, or pamphlets of any sort; the print versions are not obsolete, but they do strike digital natives as rather quaint" (Palfrey and Gasser, 2008, p. 6). Although the Palfrey and Gasser book was only written in 2008, much of what the authors present is old news by now. Yet, there are a number of take-away lessons about generational differences that might inform library research in certain settings.

Silipigni Connaway (2008) discusses some of the habits and main information service preferences of "millennials," which are relevant for library settings:

- *Immediacy*. Millennials tend to be impatient, pay less attention to spelling and grammar and have a low tolerance for complex searching. Convenience is key.
- *More choices and selectivity*. Millennials prefer multiple formats and media.
- *Collaboration and teamwork*. Millennials prefer to collaborate virtually and in person as is demonstrated in their participation in social networking sites.
- *Experiential learning*. Millennials tend to be nonlinear thinkers, which may be attributed to surfing the web.

Accordingly, Silipigni Connaway (2008) suggests several ways in which libraries can become more meaningful to this group of users, by:

- delivering resources efficiently and quickly at the point of need at the network level;
- making library catalogs easier to use;
- accommodating different discovery and access preferences;

- allowing users to personalize the interface;
- offering multiple modes of service—virtual, face-to-face and telephone;
- providing opportunities for collaboration online and in physical library spaces.

Palfrey and Gasser (2008) suggest that accuracy is another area that all users, including millennials, should pay attention to, but do not always. The importance of accuracy is growing at a very fast pace, as a direct result of so much information being available. At the same time, accuracy and quality can be easily overlooked. These are complex, often obscure concepts that can mean different things to different people. Accuracy of information on the Internet, Palfrey and Gasser (2008) point out, has a very different meaning for a surgeon who is researching the latest surgical techniques than it does for a ninth-grader writing a research paper. Markets, social norms, computer code, and even law and regulations, can have an impact on accuracy and quality (Palfrey and Gasser, 2008); however, the authors assert that "education is the best way to help digital natives manage the information-quality problem. Digital literacy is increasingly a critical skill for digital natives to learn" (2008, p. 180).

Information literacy has been, and continues to be, an area that librarians are familiar with. More recently, some librarians and educators have started to focus on "transliteracy," which incorporates new and emerging technologies and skills—"Transliteracy is the ability to read, write, and interact across a range of platforms, tools, and media from signing and orality through handwriting, print, TV, radio and film, to digital social networks" (Transliteracy Interest Group of the LITA, 2010). However, this new landscape and skill set is defined; the role of digital literacy educator is one that is familiar to many librarians. We also know that information and digital literacy teaching practices continue to face challenges about efficacy, impact, and pedagogical soundness (Tyner, 1998; Bowden and DiBenedetto, 2001; Portmann and Roush, 2004; Sanborn, 2005). Digital literacy is not just an issue for students. A recent survey by the Federal Communications Commission, *Broadband Adoption and Use in America*, found that 22 percent of respondents did not have Internet access at home because of poor digital literacy skills (Horrigan, 2010).

Given the above, what research questions might be relevant for librarians, based on what we know so far about the impact of technology on learning, writing, and critical thinking skills? And, how best to investigate these phenomena? Investigating user research behavior, especially in settings where the users are students, may be part of a larger research agenda that includes an informed approach to information and digital literacy. Qualitative approaches may include research diaries, contextual analysis of pre- and post-instruction term papers, and even analyses of librarians' teaching approaches and pedagogical application. The ramifications of understanding digital competencies go far beyond the ability to craft a sound research paper. Librarians and other educators play an important role in helping to prepare students and other learners for participation in a democratic society (Kranich, 2001). The Knight Commission's *Report on the Information Needs of Communities in a Democracy* (2009) presents 15 recommendations for meeting community information needs in a digital age, including "integrate digital and media literacy as critical elements for education at all levels through collaboration among federal, state, and local education officials"; "fund and support public libraries and other community institutions as centers of digital and media training, especially for adults"; and "engage young people in developing the digital information and communication capacities of local communities" (Knight Commission, 2009). Libraries can therefore set exploratory research agendas to be inclusive of these ideas, with an eye towards integrating best instructional and outreach practices into daily activities.

Privacy and copyright issues are not new or relevant solely to the digital era, but they are enjoying more of the spotlight in this new environment. Palfrey and Gasser (2008) make an interesting observation about digital natives and their attitudes towards privacy. "Most young people are extremely likely to leave something behind in cyberspace that will become a lot like a tattoo—something connected to them that they cannot get rid of later in life, even if they want to, without a great deal of difficulty" (p. 53). Palfrey and Gasser (2008) suggest that, astonishingly, by the time a digital native enters the workforce, there may be hundreds or thousands of digital files on the Internet about them, over which they have no control and most likely are not even aware of.

Many libraries, especially academic libraries, have programs and literature to educate users about privacy and copyright matters. Many librarians will also tell you that much of the literature and programming around these issues are ignored, until someone lands in trouble. Privacy and copyright are obviously two different concerns, and libraries tend to be more focused on the latter of the two. One sobering point made by Palfrey and Gasser (2008, p. 73) has to do with the blind trust that society seems to have when operating in the online environment. "We as societies are relying heavily, even more than we realize, on trust—of third parties we don't know well at all" to store and guard personal information that we share online. Once again, education seems to be the way forward in terms of modeling best practices for digital natives. Parents, teachers, and technology companies (Palfrey and Gasser, 2008) all have a role to play. Librarians also fit into this matrix, since both physical and virtual library spaces may be where students first encounter serious challenges, especially with regard to copyright.

In addition, academia provides a familiar backdrop from which to study the intersection of research habits and privacy. Silipigni Connaway (2008) noted an interesting concern of a graduate student with regard to virtual reference services: "I always worry that [chat sessions] are being saved . . . if the department would get a report about what questions [I asked]." A recent PEW Internet & American Life Project survey (2010a) suggests that privacy concerns are manifest differently by the youngest of today's technology users, the group of young adults that are now and will become the heaviest of information users. "New social norms that reward disclosure are already in place among the young. The experts also expressed hope that society will be more forgiving of those whose youthful mistakes are on display in social media such as Facebook picture albums or YouTube videos" (PEW Internet & American Life Project, 2010a). These same experts also suggest that "new definitions of 'private' and 'public' information are taking shape in networked society" and that, although "millennials might change the kinds of personal information they share as they age, but the aging process will not fundamentally change the incentives to share" (PEW Internet & American Life Project, 2010a).

The state of the research and academic library

The question that is still being asked by many librarians and others is: What is the future of the library? Without a crystal ball, we just do not have the answer to that yet, and, since the question is rhetorical in nature, the answer will continue to elude us. That particular question has been asked in a number of different ways, for a very, very long time now, although we tend to think of it as strictly being tied to the recent digital changes in the environment. As far back as 1949, Coney et al. (1949) discussed the future of the academic library. Researchers have also talked about methods to gather data to address this question—for example, Wennerberg (1972) and Saunders (2009) discuss using the Delphi technique to plan the future of libraries. There are bibliographies on the subject (Sapp, 2002), and far too many articles to count (Crawford and Gorman, 1995; Wainright, 1996; Harvey, 2009; Osif, 2008; Ross and Sennyey, 2008; Shuman, 1989, 1997). Given this, does it make sense to take this on as part of a research agenda within any given library? That all depends. Certainly, the future of libraries of all types is still of great concern; hence the continued efforts by researchers to publish on the topic. Familiarity with the literature can provide a framework for identifying very specific library research that can benefit users. The research library in particular has been the topic of much speculation about its future.

In the report *No Brief Candle: Reconceiving Research Libraries for the 21st Century*, the Council on Library and Information Resources (CLIR) (2008) outlines several areas for research libraries to consider moving forward. The report, which by now is somewhat dated, represents a broader contextual landscape for academic and research libraries, wherein identity, purpose, and future utility are greatly debated and discussed. The report does touch on a number of areas that remain highly relevant for libraries and constitute some interesting areas for further exploration. Aspects related to preservation, scholarly communications, teaching, collaboration, scholarly publishing, relationships with faculty, librarian identity, and and digital technologies are considered. Internationally, organizations such as the Joint Information Systems Committee, the Research Information Network (RIN), the Research Libraries UK (RLUK), the Research Libraries Network (RLN), and the Society of College, National and University Libraries (SCONUL) are collaborating to provide consultation and leadership for academic and research libraries in order to form a "fresh focus and formulate strategies to ensure the sector continues to be a leading global force" (RIN, 2010).

ACRL (2010, p. 286) lists the top ten trends impacting the academic library as follows:

- Academic library collection growth is driven by patron demand and will include new resource types.
- Budget challenges will continue and libraries will evolve as a result.
- Changes in higher education will require that librarians possess diverse skill sets.
- Demands for accountability and assessment will increase.
- Digitization of unique library collections will increase and require a larger share of resources.
- Explosive growth of mobile devices and applications will drive new services.
- Increased collaboration will expand the role of the library within the institution and beyond.
- Libraries will continue to lead efforts to develop scholarly communication and intellectual property services.
- Technology will continue to change services and required skills.
- The definition of the library will change as physical space is repurposed and virtual space expands.

In 2007, ACRL published the top ten assumptions about the future of academic libraries and librarians:

- There will be an increased emphasis on digitizing collections, preserving digital archives, and improving methods of data storage and retrieval.
- The skill set for librarians will continue to evolve in response to the needs and expectations of the changing populations (students and faculty) that they serve.
- Students and faculty will increasingly demand faster and greater access to services.
- Debates about intellectual property will become increasingly common in higher education.
- The demand for technology-related services will grow and require additional funding.
- Higher education will increasingly view the institution as a business.
- Students will increasingly view themselves as customers and consumers, expecting high-quality facilities and services.
- Distance learning will be an increasingly more common option in higher education, and will coexist but not threaten the traditional bricks-and-mortar model.
- Free public access to information stemming from publicly funded research will continue to grow.
- Privacy will continue to be an important issue in librarianship. (Allen, Mullins and Hufford, 2007)

Each of these topics represents areas that can be explored further in a variety of ways, at the same time, each of these topics has been covered at great length in the literature already. Librarians might use information on trends and recent developments within the research library setting to make connections to observations and data they already have about their users. A good example of this is mobile technology. There is no longer any question about users' preference for ways to access information efficiently from wherever they are, and, in many cases, this access involves a mobile device. Some libraries have begun to experiment with mobile-enabled library websites; others still wonder if it is really necessary to meet user need in this way.

One interesting development in terms of exploring the future of the research library is the use of scenarios—a decidedly qualitative way to collect and analyze data. Scenarios are more commonly found within usabilty and interface evaluation settings (Isaac et al., 2008), but in this case the use of scenarios is a little different. Scenarios in this sense are mostly used within business settings to help employees brainstorm, but they can be used by any organization. A scenario is essentially a story "about how the future might unfold for our organizations, our communities and our world. Scenarios are not predictions. Rather, they are provocative and plausible accounts of how relevant external forces—such as the future political environment, scientific and technological developments, social dynamics, and economic conditions— might interact and evolve, providing our organizations with different challenges and opportunities" (Global Business Network, 2010). Library scenarios are not new—Giesecke (1998) edited a volume titled *Scenario Planning for Libraries*, and Dugan and Hernon (2002) used scenarios to highlight the importance of library policy. Authors have also written about scenarios that detail the death of the library (Putnam et al., 2004). The Association of Research Libraries (ARL, 2010) recently embarked on a project to help research library administrators set their libraries up for maximum success, using this technique:

These scenarios will capture broad environmental drivers affecting research libraries. Each scenario will tell a different plausible story that starts at the current state and takes the reader out into highly divergent future situations of research libraries, rather than detailing what research libraries might look like organizationally. Future scenarios will highlight and deepen understanding of the social, technological, economic, political/regulatory, and environmental driving forces impacting research libraries in the future. (ARL, 2010)

The public library system of New South Wales also used scenarios as a collective, experiential, and holistic approach to developing strategy, by way of "imagination and analysis" (Library Council of New South Wales, 2010, p. 6).

Although hardly a trend, the turn away from the traditional methods for exploring future direction and strategy—by committee, collection of data from canned, commercial surveys, SWOT analysis, "environmental scanning, extrapolations of past trends, or individual forecasting" (ARL, 2010)—towards a more organic and qualitative method is intriguing at best. Librarians can certainly keep tabs on the progress of these two projects and others as they emerge, to determine whether such an approach might be useful.

Understanding the role of technology through research

Curious about the cloud

Cloud computing represents an approach to data access and storage that came into the spotlight starting in the 1980s. There are many definitions out there, but for the most part cloud computing designates the ability of the user to store, access, and manipulate data regardless of the device they are using, or where they are, by way of the Internet. Knorr and Gruman (2008) suggest that cloud computing is just "virtual servers available over the Internet." Chudnov (2010) reminds us that cloud computing is hardly new; it is, however, much more trendy right now: "It's strange to watch something you've taken for granted for years suddenly become 'a thing.' Cloud computing is definitely a thing now, but it's not new and it's not even novel" (p. 33). NIST (National Institutes of Standards and Technology) defines cloud computing as "a model for enabling convenient, on-demand network access to a shared pool of configurable computing resources (e.g., networks, servers, storage, applications, and services) that can be rapidly provisioned and released with minimal management effort or service provider interaction. This cloud model promotes availability and is composed of five essential characteristics, three service models, and four deployment models" (Mell and Grance, 2009).

The PEW Internet & American Life Project (2010b, p. 2) suggests that "among the most popular cloud services now are social networking sites (the 500 million people using Facebook are being social in the cloud), webmail services like Hotmail and Yahoo mail, microblogging and blogging services such as Twitter and WordPress, video-sharing sites like YouTube, picture-sharing sites such as Flickr, document and applications sites like Google Docs, social-bookmarking sites like Delicious, business sites like eBay, and ranking, rating, and commenting sites such as Yelp and TripAdvisor". In a survey, the PEW Internet & American Life Project (2010b) found that 56 percent of Internet users use webmail; 34 percent store photos online; and 29 percent use online applications such as GoogleDocs.

There are different cloud computing service models. Software (SaaS), Platform (PaaS) and Infrastructure (IaaS) can all be delivered as services via the cloud, whereas previously these elements were physically bound to the desktop or server. The choices for service providers are also increasing, with some of the better-known applications being household names. Amazon's S3 service allows for data storage, and EC2 allows developers to run computing resources on Amazon's platform (Amazon, 2010). Zoho (2010) is an online suite of cloud "productivity and collaboration apps." Google provides a suite of applications that operate in the cloud, including Gmail, Google Docs, Google Wave, Google Calendar, Google Groups, Google Sites, and Google Video (Google, 2010), as well as a developers' application called Google App Engine.

Librarians have also started to ask how cloud computing can benefit their institutions and their users (Chudnov, 2010; Hastings, 2009; Buck, 2009; Breeding, 2009). Breeding (2009) states "cloud computing offers for libraries many interesting possibilities that may help reduce technology costs and increase capacity, reliability, and performance for some types of automation activities. Cloud computing has made strong inroads into other commercial sectors and is now beginning to find more traction in the library technology sector" (p. 22).

Repositories, storage, collaborative research and publishing, collaborative teaching, catalogs, and metadata are all elements of library services which represent ways in which libraries can take advantage of cloud computing. "OCLC probably ranks as the most prominent example of cloud computing in the library arena. The WorldCat platform involves a globally distributed infrastructure that involves the largest scale library-specific implementation" (Breeding, 2009, p. 26). User-generated content such as that found on Facebook, online photo applications, Twitter, blogs, wikis, and YouTube is indicative of a trend that indicates a certain level of comfort with relinquishing some degree of control over content. In many cases, cloud computing represents a scalable and less expensive way to provide a host of services.

For many libraries, however, it can seem like a leap of faith. Complicating the use of cloud computing are issues related to data security, privacy, bandwidth, compatibility, and quality of service (Anderson and Rainie, 2010). If a user's data is not on their desktop, it is someplace else, and someone has to be responsible for its integrity and security. For these reasons, this particular topic is an excellent area for further exploration for librarians who are curious. Qualitative and quantitative data would be helpful. Qualitative data could include feedback from users about how they feel about storing their information and data in the cloud; quantitative data might include data about which devices users typically use to access their information on the go. Cloud computing application within libraries also has financial, infrastructure, and staffing considerations, so it stands to reason that the more that librarians can learn about the challenges and benefits associated with its use, the better. As Breeding suggests,

> The days of each library operating its own local servers have largely passed. This approach rarely represents the best use of library space and personnel. As libraries develop the next phase of their technology strategies, it's important to think beyond the locally maintained computer infrastructure that increasingly represents an outdated and inefficient model. Colocation, remote hosting, virtualization, SaaS, and cloud computing each offers opportunities for libraries to expend fewer resources on maintaining infrastructure and to focus more on activities with direct benefit on library services. (2009, p. 26)

Going mobile

Mobile technology is another area that consistently creates a sense of possibility in terms of supporting the user experience. Some libraries have found a way to integrate mobile technology into their landscape, not as an afterthought, but as a priority. Users who access information by way of cell phone/PDA represent a quickly growing segment of the population, and they are library users as well. Wireless devices are also growing in number and type—smartphones, Droids, the iTouch, iPad, and iPhone, Kindle, Sony eReader, and so on—are all wireless devices that are popular. Interactions with these devices can be textual, visual, or auditory in nature, and users may be involved in different types of interactions at any one time.

According to the PEW Internet & American Life Project (2010c), 59% of all Americans now go online wirelessly, using a laptop, cellphone or PDA. There has been a noticeable increase in the types of activities wireless users engage in:

- 54% have used their mobile device to send someone a photo or video
- 23% have accessed a social networking site using their phone
- 20% have used their phone to watch a video
- 15% have posted a photo or video online
- 11% have purchased a product using their phone
- 11% have made a charitable donation by text message
- 10% have used their mobile phone to access a status update service such as Twitter

Another interesting finding from the PEW report has to do with the demographics related to wireless and particularly cell phone/PDA use. African-Americans and Latinos are wireless users in large numbers (64 percent and 63 percent respectively), and 87 percent of African-Americans and Latinos own a cellphone (PEW Internet & American Life Project, 2010c). What are users doing in mobile environments? They are searching for content, locations, multimedia, using applications such as Google Mobile. They are managing their mobile content using services like Zinadoo and Mobifeeds, and transcoding data using sites like Skweezer. They are looking for content using spoken search (Voicebox); personalizing searches using services like Stumbleupon; and using SMS-Web texting services like Google SMS and Joopz.

For the average library, going mobile requires technological expertise, human resources, and financial commitment. It can be unclear if the benefits to users are worth the effort. Exploring the possible ways to integrate mobile technology is certainly a research area that is highly relevant today. Librarians and others have been dabbling in this area for a long time now, trying to figure out what going mobile might mean for libraries (Fox, 2002, 2003, 2004, 2005). A random virtual visit to a cross-section of library websites via your mobile device will produce information that is often unreadable, unloadable, and unusable. It is not just libraries that do not provide mobile-enabled access—many sites on the web just are not there yet. In a recent survey of 111 Association of Research Libraries (ARL) members' university websites, 39 were mobile-enabled, and out of those 39, 14 libraries had mobile-enabled presentation for some segments of their websites (Aldrich, 2010). Despite the fact that most libraries do not have web-enabled content, libraries of all types *are* adding mobile-enabled websites to their information landscape, including American University, Harvard University, Regina Public Library, and New York Public Library.

The matrix: a tool for the beginning

There are many different paths that lead to discovery, and library research is no different. How can librarians and others combine strategic plans, research agendas, current developments, and user need to come up with research questions that are relevant to their jobs, and executable in terms of methodology? It is not an easy task, especially if librarians are interested in a more qualitative approach. There are a few guidelines for collecting quantitative data and their evaluation. For instance, the International Federation of Library Associations and Institutions (IFLA) produced a matrix which lists the research topic, types of data to collect, definitions, and how to count the data (IFLA, 2007; see Figure 4.1).

Librarians can create their own matrix to help stimulate discussion during the brainstorming phase. Table 4.1 provides an example of one way to begin visualizing all the many questions and elements that can help to build a research framework, regardless of the approach. This matrix can be reorganized and filled in any order—the point is to get librarians and researchers in any given setting talking about the things that are important to users, the connection to library goals, and the ways in which research can identify challenges, problems, and, most importantly, opportunities. It is not meant to be a formal exercise— informal discussions with notes on newsprint or a blackboard will do just fine.

As is the case with exploring any new technology or new service, it is important for researchers to get out and experience how other libraries and information spaces have interpreted and met user need by way of research practices. Research can tell us a lot about certain aspects, but it cannot tell us everything.

Figure 4.1 Information Resource Data Collection

	Topic	Data	Definitions (ISO 278, partly adapted)	How to count
Resources for information access (passive availability)	Collection	**Collection size** (volumes)	**volume** = physical unit for a printed document assembling a certain number of leaves under one cover to form a whole or part of set	Count the number of printed documents (books and bound volumes of serials) in the collection at the end of the year.
		Number of electronic serials (subscriptions)	**electronic serial** = serial published in electronic form only or in both electronic and another format NOTE 1 Comprises serials held locally and remote resources for which access rights have been acquired, at least for a certain period of time. NOTE 2 Open access journals (free Internet resources) are excluded	Count the number of subscriptions to electronic journals and newspapers at the end of the year. Include titles acquired for remote access and additional electronic licenses for access to titles held in print format. Include titles comprised in "additional access" or "cross access" in consortia agreements for the time of the contractual agreement. Exclude electronic journals that are free on the Internet.
		Number of e-books (titles)	**e-book** = digital document, licensed or not, where searchable text is prevalent, and which can be seen in analogy to a print book (monograph)	Count the number of purchased or licensed e-books (titles) in the collection at the end of the year. The number of titles can be higher than the number of subscriptions, as there may be several titles comprised in one E-book.
		Number of databases	**database** = collection of electronically stored descriptive records or content units (including facts, full texts, pictures, and sound) with a common user interface and software for the retrieval and manipulation of the data	Count the number of purchased or licensed databases in the collection at the end of the year. This includes databases on the local network or installed on stand-alone workstations and on other servers where the library has acquired access rights at least for a certain period of time.
	Library as physical place	**Number of user workplaces** (seats)	**seats** = seat provided for users for reading or studying, whether with or without equipment NOTE Includes seats in carrels, in seminar and study rooms and the audiovisual and children's departments of the library. Excludes seats in halls, lecture and auditory theaters intended for audiences of special events. Also excludes floor space on which users may sit and similar informal seating.	Count the number of seats available in the library to users at the end of the year.

Source: IFLA (2007).

| Table 4.1 | Matrix for Use during the Brainstorming Phase | | |

Want to explore . . .	In order to . . .	Possible resources	Possible research approaches
Cloud computing	Enhance the flexible work and storage space of library users; support the storage and dissemination of large datasets	Survey of the professional literature in information and computing science	Collect qualitative data on scholarly publishing and access at the institution; quantitative data on robustness of existing cloud-based repositories, applications, and services
Graduate students' literature review practices for their dissertations	Enhance library research services, repository, and faculty connections	Survey of the professional literature	Research diaries, periodic interviews

References

Aldrich, A. (2010) Universities and libraries move to the mobile web. *EDUCAUSE Quarterly*, 33(2). Retrieved from *http://www.educause.edu/EDUCAUSE+Quarterly/EDUCAUSEQuarterlyMagazineVolum/Universitiesand LibrariesMoveto/206531*.

Allen, F.R., Mullins, J.L. and Hufford, J.R. (2007) Top ten assumptions for the future of academic libraries and librarians: A report from the ACRL research committee. Retrieved from *https://wendolene.tosm.ttu.edu/handle/2346/493*.

Amazon (2010) Retrieved from *http://aws.amazon.com/ec2/*.

Anderson, J. and Rainie, L. (2010) Pew Internet & American Life Project Report: The future of the internet, social networking, communities: The future of social relations. Retrieved from *http://pewinternet.org/~/media//Files/Reports/2010/PIP_Future_of_Internet_%202010_social_relations.pdf.*

Association of College & Research Libraries (ACRL) (2010) 2010 top ten trends in academic libraries: A review of the current literature. *College & Research Libraries News,* 71(6): 286–92.

Association of Research Libraries (ARL) (2010) Retrieved from *http://www.arl.org/rtl/plan/scenarios/index.shtml.*

Bennett, S., Maton, K. and Kervin, L. (2008) The "digital natives" debate: A critical review of the evidence. *British Journal of Educational Technology,* 39(5): 775–86.

Bowden, T.S. and DiBenedetto, A. (2001) Information literacy in a biology laboratory session: An example of librarian-faculty collaboration. *Research Strategies,* 18(2): 143–9.

Breeding, M. (2009) The advance of computing from the ground to the cloud. *Computers in Libraries,* November/December. Retrieved from *http://www.librarytechnology.org/ltg-displaytext.pl?RC=14384.*

Brown, J.S. (2002) Growing up digital: How the web changes work, education, and the ways people learn. *Education at a Distance USDLA Journal.* Retrieved from *http://www.usdla.org/html/journal/FEB02_Issue/article01.html.*

Buck, S. (2009) Libraries in the cloud: Making a case for Google and Amazon. *Computers in Libraries,* 29(8): 6–10.

Carlson, S. (2005) The net generation goes to college. *Chronicle of Higher Education,* October 7. Retrieved from *http://chronicle.com/free/v52/i07/07a03401.htm.*

Chudnov, D. (2010) A view from the clouds. *Computers in Libraries,* 30(3): 33–5.

Coney, D., McKeon, N.F. and Branscomb, B.H. (1949) The future of libraries in academic institutions. *Harvard Library Bulletin.*

Connaway, L.S. (2008) Make room for the Millennials. *NextSpace*, 10, 18–19. Retrieved from *http://www.oclc.org/nextspace/010/research.htm.*

Council on Library and Information Resources (CLIR) (2008) No brief candle: Reconceiving research libraries for the 21st century. Retrieved from *http://www.clir.org/pubs/reports/pub142/pub142.pdf.*

Crawford, W. and Gorman, M. (1995) *Future Libraries: Dreams, Madness & Reality.* Chicago, IL: American Library Association.

Dugan, R.E. and Hernon, P. (2002) Outcomes assessment: not synonymous with inputs and outputs. *Journal of Academic Librarianship*, 28(6): 376–80.

Facer, K. and Furlong, R. (2001) Beyond the myth of the "Cyberkid": Young people at the margins of the information revolution. *Journal of Youth Studies*, 4(4): 451–69.

Fox, M. (2002) PDAs and handhelds in libraries. Presentation given at ACRL/NEC Conference, January 15, 2002. Retrieved from *http://web.simmons.edu/~fox/pda/.*

Fox, M. (2003) PDAs in academic libraries: We've got the whole world in our palms. Presentation given at State University of New York Librarians Association (SUNYLA) 35th Annual Conference. June 4, 2003, Stony Brook, NY. Retrieved from *http://web.simmons.edu/~fox/pda/.*

Fox, M. (2004) PDAs in libraries. Presentation given at Computer in Libraries, Washington, DC, March 12, 2004. Retrieved from *http://web.simmons.edu/~fox/pda/.*

Fox, M. (2005) Building communities in the "palm" of your hand. Presentation given at Computer in Libraries,

Washington, DC, March 17, 2005. Retrieved from *http:// web.simmons.edu/~fox/pda/*.

Frand, J. (2000) The information-age mindset: changes in students and implications for higher education. *EDUCAUSE Review*, 35: 14–24.

Giesecke, J. (1998) *Scenario Planning for Libraries*. Chicago, IL: American Library Association.

Global Business Network (GBN) (2010) Retrieved from *http://www.gbn.com/about/scenario_planning.php*.

Google (2010) Retrieved from *www.google.com/apps*.

Green, B., Reid, J. and Bigum, C. (2003) Teaching the Nintendo generation: Children, computer culture and popular technologies. In: S. Howard (ed.), *Wired-up: Young people and the electronic media* (pp. 19–42). London: Routledge.

Harvey, S. (2009) *The Future of Libraries Without Walls*. London: Facet Publishing.

Hastings, R. (2009) Cloud computing. *Library Technology Reports*, 45(4).

Helsper, E.J. (2008) *Digital inclusion: An analysis of social disadvantage and the information society*. London, Department of Communities and Local Government. Retrieved from *http://www.communities.gov.uk/documents/ communities/pdf/digitalinclusionsummary*.

Horrigan, J.B. (2010) *Broadband adoption and use in America*. Federal Communications Commission. Retrieved from *http://online.wsj.com/public/resources/documents/ FCCSurvey.pdf*.

Howe, N. and Strauss, W. (2003) *Millennials go to College*. Washington, DC: American Association of Collegiate Registrars and Admissions Officers.

International Federation of Library Associations and Institutions (IFLA) (2007) Global statistics for the 21st century. Retrieved from *http://archive.ifla.org/VII/s22/ project/GlobalStatistics.htm*.

Isaac, A., Matthezing, H., van der Meij, L., Schlobach, L., Wang, S. and Zinn, C. (2008) Putting ontology alignment in context: Usage scenarios, deployment and evaluation in a library case. *Lecture Notes in Computer Science*, 5021/2008, 402–17.

Jamali, H.R. and Nicholas, D. (2010) Interdisciplinarity and the information-seeking behavior of scientists. *Information Processing and Management*, 46(2): 233–43.

Jukes, L., McCain, I. and Crockett, T. (2010) *Understanding the Digital Generation: Teaching and learning in the new digital landscape*. New York, NY: Corwin Press.

Knight Commission Report (2009) Retrieved from *http://www.knightcomm.org/recommendations/*.

Knorr, E. and Gruman, G. (2008) What cloud computing really means. *InfoWorld*, April 7, 2008. Retrieved from *http://www.infoworld.com/d/cloud-computing/what-cloud-computing-really-means-031*.

Kranich, N. (ed.) (2001) *Libraries and Democracy: The Cornerstones of Liberty*. Chicago, IL: American Library Association.

Levin, D. and Arafeh, S. (2002) The digital disconnect: the widening gap between Internet-savvy students and their schools. Washington, DC: Pew Internet & American Life Project. Retrieved from *http://www.pewinternet.org/report_display.asp?r=67*.

Levin, D., Richardson, J. and Arafeh, S. (2002) Digital disconnect: students' perceptions and experiences with the internet and education. In P. Baker and S. Rebelsky (eds.), *Proceedings of ED-MEDIA, World Conference on Educational Multimedia, Hypermedia and Telecommunications*, 51–2. Norfolk, VA: Association for the Advancement of Computing in Education.

Library Council of New South Wales (2010) Retrieved from *http://www.sl.nsw.gov.au/services/public_libraries/publications/docs/bookendsscenarios.pdf*.

Long, S.A. (2005) What's new in libraries? Digital natives: if you aren't one, get to know one. *New Library World*, 106(3/4): 187.

Mell, P. and Grance, T. (2009) The NIST definition of cloud computing. National Institute of Standards and Technology, Information Technology Laboratory, ver. 15. Retrieved from *csrc.nist.gov/groups/SNS/cloud-computing/cloud-def-v15.doc*.

Nicholas, D., Huntington, P., Jamali, H., Rowlands, I. and Fieldhouse, M. (2009) Student digital information-seeking behaviour in context. *Journal of Documentation*, 65(1): 106–32.

Oblinger, D. (2003) Boomers, Gen-Xers and Millennials: Understanding the new students. *EDUCAUSE Review*, 38(4): 37–47.

Oblinger, D. and Oblinger, J. (2005) Is it age or IT: first steps towards understanding the net generation. In D. Oblinger and J. Oblinger (eds), *Educating the Net generation* (pp. 2.1–2.20). Boulder, CO: EDUCAUSE.

Online Computer Library Center (OCLC) (2010) Retrieved from *http://www.oclc.org/research/*.

Osif, B.A. (2008) W(h)ither libraries? The future of libraries, part 1. *Library Administration and Management*, 22, 49–54.

Palfrey, J. and Gasser, U. (2008) *Born Digital: Understanding the First Generation of Digital Natives*. New York: Basic Books.

PEW Internet & American Life Project (2010a) Retrieved from *http://pewresearch.org/pubs/1660/internet-experts-say-aging-millennials-will-continue-personal-disclosure-information-sharing*.

PEW Internet & American Life Project (2010b) Retrieved from *http://www.pewinternet.org/~/media//Files/Reports/2010/PIP_Future_of_the_Internet_cloud_computing.pdf*.

PEW Internet & American Life Project (2010c) Retrieved from *http://pewresearch.org/pubs/1654/wireless-internet-users-cell-phone-mobile-data-applications*.

Portmann, C. and Roush, A.J. (2004) Assessing the effects of library instruction. *Journal of Academic Librarianship*, 30(6): 461–65.

Prendiville, T.W., Saunders, J. and Fitzsimons, J. (2009) The information-seeking behaviour of paediatricians accessing web-based resources. *Archives of Disease in Childhood*, 94(8): 633–5.

Prensky, M. (2001) Digital natives, digital immigrants part 1. *On the Horizon*, 9(5): 1–6.

Prensky, M. (2005) Engage me or enrage me. *EDUCAUSE Review*, 40(5): 61–4.

Putnam, R., Feldstein, L.M. and Cohen, D. (2004) *Better Together: Restoring the American Community*. New York: Simon & Schuster.

Pyati, A. (2003) Limited English proficient users and the need for improved reference services. *Reference Services Review*, 31(3): 264–71.

Radford, M.L. and Snelson, P. (2009) *Academic Library Research: Perspectives and current trends*. Chicago, IL: Association of College and Research Libraries, A Division of the American Library Association.

Research Information Network (RIN) (2010) Retrieved from *http://www.rin.ac.uk/our-work/using-and-accessing-information-resources/towards-academic-library-future*.

Rosen, L. (2010) *Rewired: Understanding the iGeneration and the Way They Learn*. New York: Palgrave Macmillan.

Ross, L. and Sennyey, P. (2008) The library is dead, long live the library! The practice of academic librarianship and the digital revolution. *Journal of Academic Librarianship*, 34(2): 145–52.

Rushkoff, D. (1996) *Playing the Future: How kids' culture can teach us to thrive in an age of chaos.* New York: HarperCollins.

Sanborn, L. (2005) Improving library instruction: Faculty collaboration. *Journal of Academic Librarianship*, 31(5): 477–81.

Sapp, G. (2002) *A Brief History of the Future of Libraries: An Annotated Bibliography.* Lanham, MD: Scarecrow Press.

Saunders, L. (2009) The future of information literacy in academic libraries: A Delphi Study. *Portal: Libraries and the Academy*, 9(1): 99–114.

Shuman, B.A. (1989) *The Library of the Future: Alternative Scenarios for the Information Profession.* Englewood, CO: Libraries Unlimited.

Shuman, B.A. (1997) *Beyond the Library of the Future: More Alternative Futures for the Public Library.* Englewood, CO: Libraries Unlimited.

Tapscott, D. (1998) *Growing up Digital: The Rise of the Net Generation.* New York: McGraw-Hill.

Tapscott, D. (2008) *Grown up Digital: How the Net Generation is Changing Your World.* New York: McGraw-Hill.

Timmers, C.F. and Glas, C.A.W. (2010) Developing scales for information-seeking behaviour. *Journal of Documentation*, 66(1): 46–69.

Transliteracy Interest Group of the American Library Association (2010) Retrieved from *http://connect.ala.org/transliteracy*.

Tyner, K. (1998) *Literacy in a Digital World: Teaching and Learning in the Age of Information.* New Jersey: Lawrence Erlbaum and Associates.

Wainright, E. (1996) Digital libraries: Some implications for government and education from the Australian development experience. Paper presented at Singapore, 1996. National Library of Australia Staff Papers. Retrieved from *http://www-prod.nla.gov.au/openpublish/index.php/ nlasp/article/viewArticle/1004/1274*.

Wennerberg, U. (1972) Using the Delphi Technique for planning the future libraries. *Unesco Bulletin for Libraries*, 26(5): 242–6.

Wildemuth, B.M. (2002) Effective methods for studying information seeking and use. *Journal of the American Society for Information Science and Technology*, 1218–22.

Zoho (2010) Retrieved from *http://www.zoho.com/*.

5

Inside the mind of the user: qualitative approaches to understanding user experience in library settings

Abstract: This chapter focuses on the use of qualitative approaches as a way to understand user experience in library environments. A definition of user experience is provided, as well as discussion about design thinking and consideration of "flow" in terms of the user experience. The role of research in consumer-driven markets is also discussed as a way to illustrate the concept.

Key words: user experience, design thinking, flow, Ed Bernays, Csikszentmihalyi, William Gribbons.

Any given library can provide users with a wide range of experiences. There is the discovery experience, the searching experience, the reference experience, the studying experience. Users may also encounter the lost experience, the anxious experience, the overwhelming experience, or any combination of hundreds of others. There is no way to record and make sense of every single user experience—and why would anyone want to do that anyway? Enhancing the user's experience, whatever it is, is a very important factor for libraries of all types to consider. In order to enhance the experience, we first need to know more about it, and that is where qualitative research comes in.

This chapter presents an overview of user experience as a concept for exploring the relationship between end users and the environments, products, or services they interact with—in this case, the library or information service setting. UX, as it is commonly referred to, has great potential in terms of determining improvements for user services within library and information contexts. UX research can be facilitated in a number of ways, and this chapter will discuss some qualitative approaches. User experience is relevant now because there is, more than ever before, a greater focus on the needs of the user, as opposed to a narrower focus on resources, products, or services. In other words, looking for, finding, and applying information in any form are "experiences" that are now had by many. It stands to reason that librarians and others who help users on a daily basis look for ways to improve the nature of these experiences.

User experience is not a new concept, but it has become more popular within the past ten years or so. Usability experts recognize it within the context of graphic interface and web design, as a way to measure the degree of impact on the end user. UX is actually a much broader concept, currently being examined within the context of the human experience in a wide variety of environments. Experience, generally speaking, comprises certain elements—direct observations, practical knowledge, perception, and conscious events. William Gribbons, Director for the Human Factors graduate program at Bentley College in Massachusetts, thinks about UX this way:

> The user experience is the careful alignment of human behaviors, needs, and abilities with the core value delivered through a product or service. Depending on context, this experience may have psychological, cultural, physiological, and emotional components—or a combination of the four.

We define the optimum experience through detailed study and assessment of "people" in the appropriate user environment. (Gribbons, 2009)

Peter Morville (2004) describes the facets of the user experience as those that provide information that is useful, usable, desirable, findable, accessible, credible, and valuable. There are lots of other definitions out there, but the combination of Morville (2004) and Gribbons (2009) really provides a holistic view of what UX means.

Gribbons (2009) helps us understand the relatively recent focus on UX by suggesting that there are four drivers. A shift to the "experience economy" as defined by Pine and Gilmore (1999); more competition in the marketplace and the heightened need for differentiation; the applicability of understanding the user across a wide variety of sectors; and the potential of UX design to help create better services, products, and environments. There are four broadly defined categories that all play a role in how we experience design of any sort—emotional (Bernays, 1969; Norman, 2005, 2009), cultural (Bernays, 1969; Norman, 2005, 2009; Pine and Gilmore, 1999), psychological (Cushman, 1995; Csikszentmihalyi, 1981, 1990, 1994, 1996, 1998), and physiological (Westerink et al., 2009). Each of these areas must produce a positive effect in order for us to feel that we have had a great experience.

The self and user experience

Sigmund Freud (1923) helped to define how we see our innermost drives, emotions, and behaviors. The idea of the self and all of its representations remains central to every major area of human development. It is a very intriguing idea, with some interesting connections to the user experience. In the 1920s, Edward Bernays, Freud's nephew, began to explore ways to manipulate (for lack of a better word) the unconscious for the sake of driving consumer markets. Bernays is largely credited with being the father of public relations, and his strategy had not been seen before. Bernays capitalized on Freud's conceptualization of man as an irrational being driven by irrational drives that threaten to overtake him at any moment. Bernays focused on consumerism, and finding ways to convince the public of a growing need for products and services in order to feel safe, loved, productive, and worthwhile. Consumerism was a perfect way to address these so-called irrational drives and, in some ways, to control them. At its heart, Bernays' activities were based on exploiting the user experience.

Bernays' projects included work with the cigarette industry, household products and the automobile industry. Bernays' work represented more than just a play on emotions—he somehow discovered a way to tap into the unconscious fears and vulnerabilities that we all have. Think about how the consumer-driven market works today: If someone can convince you that you or your family are unsafe and vulnerable, you are much more likely to buy products and services that you think will keep you safe—even if you cannot really define the danger, or have no evidence of impending harm. These user experiences thus revolve around perceived need—the greater we think our need is for a product, the more important it is to purchase it and, usually, the more intense the user experience.

Bernays has been both criticized and lauded for his unique approach to marketing and publicity. Regardless of how manipulative this all may seem, Bernays started a trend that continues to this day. The user experience remains a central element in driving consumer markets, and the engineering of need plays a critical role.

So, what does all of this have to do with library research? Quite a bit, actually. The consumer-driven market has a definite impact on the expectations and desires of the folks who use libraries and information services. Users typically do not see libraries as any different from the consumer environments that they experience every day—those which feature immediate customer service, 24-hour access to information, personalized technology to enhance current services and products, and the best "value" for cost are all expectations that users may feel entitled to. Hernon and Altman (2010, p. vii) suggest that library users are definitely "customers," despite the fact that some librarians recoil at the use of the word. The authors further suggest that library users are not a captive audience—that there is a lot of competition for their business (Hernon and Altman, 2010). Librarians have a very long history of providing for users and, therefore, they are in the best position to "create and perfect services that better match the information needs, information-seeking behaviors, and expectations" of users (Hernon and Altman, 2010, p. ix). Sadeh (2007) reminds us of the generational impact of millennial users on the services they seek and use. Their experiences are very much colored by experiences with products and activities that they see as an essential part of their lives—whether it is social networking, web commerce, or highly personalized technology.

Design, broken-ness, and the library user experience

The "design" of the library experience is another element related to the overall user experience. Design suggests an intentional attempt to create, and the expression of some type of vision, rather than an arbitrary or unintentional occurrence. The word usually conjures up the traditional context for a design, related to creating physical, graphical, and sometimes experiential elements. In libraries, designing experience can be all of those things and more. There are quite a few resources about design and the library. *Library Journal* now features a column entitled "The User Experience" (2010) that discusses the role of design. One of the better-known resources is Steven Bell's "Designing Better Libraries" blog (*http://dbl.lishost.org/blog/*). Schmidt (2010) reminds librarians that, "whether you know it or not, you're already a designer. Every time librarians create a bookmark, decide to house a collection in a new spot, or figure out how a new service might work, they're making design decisions. This is what I like to call design by neglect or unintentional design. Whether library employees wear name tags is a design decision. The length of loan periods and whether or not you charge fines is a design decision. Anytime you choose how people will interact with your library, you're making a design decision. All of these decisions add up to create an experience, good or bad, for your patrons."

Schmidt (2010) makes some important observations about the role of those who work in libraries in designing and assessing the user experience. In any library setting, there are probably elements that have been very carefully designed, and others that have been put into place without much thought, or just have always been there. It can be difficult to try and design elements or redesign elements when it is unclear how, if, or why those elements do or do not work for users. Research can help evaluate and support design elements within any library, and help librarians and others to actually design a valuable user experience. Seth Godin, author of *Tribes* (2008) and marketing entrepreneur, challenges businesses and designers of all types to discover what is "broken," and to fix it. Bell (2008) urges library workers to use "design thinking" to create better user experiences, which includes evaluation. Beckman and Barry (2007) suggest that the application of design thinking is incredibly broad:

> It can be applied to the design and development of both hardware and software products, to the design of business models and services, to the design of organizations and how they work, and to the design of the buildings and spaces in which work takes place, or within which companies interact with their customers. (2007, p. 25)

Design thinking involves four elements: observation, framing, imperatives (the needs or underlying design principles), and solutions (Beckman and Barry, 2007). Bell (2008) elaborates on the elements of design thinking as follows:

- empathic thinking
- identifying the problem before the solution
- brainstorming process
- prototyping process
- formative/summative evaluation.

Regardless of how it is conceptualized, the bottom line is that paying attention to what does not work in your library or information setting (in other words, what is broken), and to what does work, and finding out why, is really the only way to create better user experiences—and qualitative strategies involving observation, ethnographic work, and field studies can help us to do that. As Barry and Beckman (2008) state,

Design thinking is grounded in the concrete analytical work done in the observation phase. Deeply understanding stakeholder needs—the needs of customers, users, value chain partners, as well as internal corporate requirements—through observation or ethnographic research methods lays the groundwork for the design thinking cycle. Effective observation takes in not only use- and usability-based needs, but meaning-based needs as well. (Barry and Beckman, 2008)

Findings from user experience research can then be articulated as problems to be addressed, or best practices/things that work. Design thinking can help identify and match problems to creative solutions. Gribbons (2009) also suggests that librarians consider the following when trying to create better experiences for users:

- Define and re-define the core values of the organization—these can be related to collections, populations, educational support, physical and virtual spaces.
- Decide which elements of the user experience map naturally and productively to these values.
- Explore segmentation—target specific experiences to specific groups. One size does not fit all!
- Consider all possible touch points—virtual, physical, staff, collections.

One of the most important aspects of user experience research is working to understand the user within the context of behaviors, reactions, and interactions related to their current experience. Participant observation techniques are a great way to gather this type of data, as are focus groups and interviews. Interpreting the quality or meaning of a user's experience based on these collected data can be difficult— qualitative data are certainly not as clear-cut as their quantitative partner. Barry and Beckman (2008) discuss the creating of frameworks to help figure out what it all means. "The ultimate purpose of framing is to *reframe*, to target the user's problem in a different way and ultimately come up with a new story to tell about how the solution might fix the problem" (Barry and Beckman, 2008). For librarians, this means getting at the story of our users, and seeing beyond the tasks they come to the library to undertake on any given day. Barry and Beckman (2008) provide a really nice example of how Amtrak's Acela train reframed what it meant to travel by train, by capitalizing on the fact that it gives people the time to sit back, relax, look out of the window, and watch the world go by (in a good way). The resulting promotion included the tagline "inner children travel free" (Barry and Beckman, 2008). In just a few words, customers are reminded of all the positive stories and memories from train journeys of the past, but in a modern context.

Useit.com on UX research

Jakob Nielsen is arguably one of the most recognized names when it comes to usability and interactive design. Nielsen's popular usability website Useit.com contains a lot of helpful information, including a review of what investigative methods may be best suited for a particular user experience research project. Although the focus here is on the interface, the guidelines are useful for many other types of user experiences. Rohrer (2008) suggests that research methods should be viewed across three dimensions when deciding which to use:

- *Attitudinal vs. Behavioral*—what people say vs. what they do;
- *Qualitative vs. Quantitative*—why and how to fix a problem vs. how many and how much;
- *Context of website or Product Use*—whether research participants are using or not using the product/ services. (Rohrer, 2008)

Rohrer (2008) states that "due to the nature of their differences, qualitative methods are much better suited for answering questions about why or how to fix a problem, whereas quantitative methods do a much better job answering 'how many' and 'how much' type of questions." There is also an emphasis on the nature of the user interaction, and whether the user is using the product or service, or not. A variety of data collection methods give researchers the ability to mix and match, depending on the aims of the project. Diary studies, surveys, focus groups, camera studies, and ethnographic studies can all yield qualitative data. Conceptualizing research in this way can be extremely helpful for librarians and other researchers who are interested in finding out more about the many pathways to exploring the user experience—whether the experience is related to website use, space use, or research and instructional services use. The focus is always on the experience, ways to document it, and ways to understand it.

A recent study conducted by librarians at Rutgers University (see also Chapter 6) provides a good example of a qualitative approach to understanding users' library experience. The study, conducted within the context of redesigning the library's website, used surveys and semi-structured interview data to compile an ethnography—essentially, a combination of users' research and library experience stories. The result was an incredibly detailed report, which highlighted the many facets of the student research experience—from students' aspirations, academic role models, and fears, to their everyday habits that help them to navigate the academic landscape both within and outside of the library. Understanding experience within this context is reminiscent of the University of Rochester Libraries' ethnographic study of students, which led the researchers into dormitory rooms, student homes, and other spaces on campus on their quest to understand various aspects of student life (see also Chapter 3).

Flow as an element of the user experience

With all the talk about experience, it makes sense to ask: What makes for a positive or optimal experience? There is quite a bit of literature on the topic, much of it from the psychological disciplines. Mihaly Csikszentmihalyi (1990) is well-known for introducing and studying the concept of "flow," which is closely tied to what makes for an ideal experience. The phrase "flow" comes from the participants in one of many research projects conducted by Csikszentimihalyi and his colleagues, where they talked about being in the "flow" of things. Flow is described as "a subjective experience of engaging just-manageable challenges by tackling a series of goals, continuously processing feedback about progress, and adjusting action based on this feedback. Under these conditions, experience seamlessly unfolds from moment to moment" (Csikszentmihalyi and Nakamura, 2002, p. 90). The concept of flow has been applied to many aspects of human development, including creativity (Csikszentmihalyi, 1990); work productivity (Csikszentmihalyi, 1988, 1990); learning

(Rathunde and Csikszentmihalyi, 2005); sports (Hunter and Csikszentmihalyi, 2000); religious experience (Csikszentmihalyi, 1988, 1990); music (Parncutt and McPherson, 2002); and emotional development (Rathunde and Csikszentmihalyi, 2006). It has also been studied in relation to online and multimedia experiences, namely videogames (Cowley et al., 2004).

It is mentioned here because it is an intriguing concept and some researchers believe it is the main component in the ideal experience. Within library and information settings, the concept may not be relevant across all activities, but it may be relevant for some, for example, interactive online searching (Wildemuth, 2006). The users' state of mind while engaged in online searching has been studied extensively, but there have not been as many studies looking at the aspect of "flow." Mathwick and Rigdon (2004) state that the "challenge and skill associated with online information search activity will induce a state of mind that affects experiential outcomes" (p. 324). They suggest that flow can apply to online consumer experiences, recreational, and non-recreational online experiences. In addition to defining the state of flow, Csikszentmihalyi also described four progressive states of mind and skills associated with flow (Csikszentmihalyi and Csikszentmihalyi, 1988, p. 261):

- *Flow*—Challenge and skill are balanced and elevated above some critical threshold.
- *Boredom*—Skill exceeds the level of challenge for a task.
- *Apathy*—Skill and challenge fall below a critical threshold.
- *Anxiety*—Challenge exceeds the skill level for a task.

If you think about your own information search and retrieval experiences, you may be able to identify certain times where you felt completely in the zone, finding what you needed quickly, using information to help create and support ideas, writing, and other efforts. Those times are often characterized by a feeling of complete focus, a feeling of mastery—you know what you are looking for and you are finding it—and a feeling of control. These times vary drastically from those frustrating sessions when you cannot seem to find anything that you are looking for. Users experience similar states (Palmquist and Kyung-Sun, 2000; Tsai and Tsai, 2003; Ghani and Deshpande, 1994). According to Csikszentmihalyi and Csikszentmihalyi (1988), experiencing flow is a positive and encouraging experience that bolsters a person's confidence and makes them more likely to come back for more. From a library perspective, enhancing the flow experience may be one way to enhance the user experience. That is not to say that librarians or others who work in information service environments can control this aspect of the user interaction, but there may be ways to enhance library services and products to support more effective and efficient search and retrieval, giving users more control over their search environments. Lack of control is certainly an impediment to achieving an optimal search experience (Novak et al., 2003; Novak et al., 2000), and research has demonstrated that tools such as those that allow users to personalize their information environments, and integrate services that they use on a daily basis (such as social networking), can positively impact the user experience (Detlor and Lewis, 2006; Brantley et al., 2006). These elements are worth considering in any library or information setting. Qualitative research can help reveal information about users and their optimal states—when/if they have experienced these states and under what circumstances. Finding out whether a library's current information or online tools contribute to users' feeling of flow is also important. Helping users achieve flow is not an objective here—but understanding what environmental elements within a library setting might set users up for success is a worthwhile goal. Diaries and a checklist of descriptive states while engaged in online research, search, and retrieval activities might be an intriguing way for users to describe their experiences.

Embarking on a qualitative study of the user experience does require that researchers be open to learning new things, and open to the fact that being an information or library expert does not automatically make one a user expert. Many of the little things that we may tend to ignore in everyday life count—they contribute to the overall experience in some way.

References

Barry, M. and Beckman, S. (2008) Developing design thinking capabilities. *STEP magazine*. Retrieved from *http://www.stepinsidedesign.com/STEPMagazine/Article/28885/*.

Beckman, S. and Barry, M. (2007) Innovation as a learning process: Embedding design thinking. *California Management Review*, 50(1): 25–56.

Bell, S. (2008) From customer service to user experience: Using design thinking to exceed user expectations. Presentation given at Pioneer Library System, November 21, 2008. Retrieved from *stevenbell.info/ppts/PLDprogramslides.ppt*.

Bell, S. (2010) Designing better libraries blog. Retrieved from *http://dbl.lishost.org/blog/*.

Bernays, D. (1969) The engineering of consent: A scientific approach to public relations. Retrieved from *http://classes .dma.ucla.edu/Fall07/28/Engineering_of_consent.pdf*.

Brantley, S., Armstrong, A. and Lewis, K. (2006) Usability testing of a customizable library web portal. *College and Research Libraries*, 67(2): 146–63.

Cowley, B., Charles, D., Black, M. and Hickey, R. (2008) Toward an understanding of flow in video games. *Computers in Entertainment (CIE)*, 6(2): 1–27.

Csikszentmihalyi, M. (1981) *The Meaning of Things: Domestic Symbols and the Self*. Cambridge: Cambridge University Press.

Csikszentmihalyi, M. (1990) *Flow: The Psychology of Optimal Experience*. New York: Harper and Row.

Csikszentmihalyi, M. (1994) *The Evolving Self*. New York: HarperPerennial.

Csikszentmihalyi, M. (1996) *Creativity: Flow and the Psychology of Discovery and Invention*. New York: HarperPerennial.

Csikszentmihalyi, M. (1998) *Finding Flow: The Psychology of Engagement with Everyday Life*. New York: Basic Books.

Csikszentmihalyi, M. and Csikszentmihalyi, I. (1988) *Optimal Experience: Psychological Studies of Flow in Consciousness*. Cambridge: Cambridge University Press.

Csikszentimihalyi, M. and Nakamura, J. (2002) The concept of flow. In C.R. Snyder and S. López (eds), *Handbook of positive psychology* (pp. 89–105). Oxford: Oxford University Press.

Cushman, P. (1995) *Constructing the Self, Constructing America: A Cultural History of Psychotherapy*. Reading, MA: Addison-Wesley.

Detlor, B. and Lewis, V. (2006) Academic library websites: Current practice and future directions. *Journal of Academic Librarianship*, 32(3): 251–8.

Freud, S. (1923) *The Ego and the Id*. London: Hogarth Press Ltd.

Ghani, J. and Deshpande, S. (1994) Task characteristics and the experience of optimal flow in human-computer interaction. *Journal of Psychology*, 128(4): 381–91.

Godin, S. (2008) *Tribes*. New York: Portfolio Hardcover.

Gribbons, W. (2009) From transaction to interaction: Transforming the user experience. Presentation at Memorial Sloan Kettering Hospital, April 24, 2009, New York.

Hernon, P. and Altman, E. (2010) *Assessing Service Quality: Satisfying the Expectations of Library Customers*. Chicago, IL: American Library Association.

Hunter, J. and Csikszentmihalyi, M. (2000) The phenomenology of body-mind: The contrasting cases of flow in sports and contemplation. *Anthropology of Consciousness*, 11(3–4): 15.

Library Journal (2010) User experience column. Retrieved from *http://www.libraryjournal.com/article/CA6713142 .html*.

Mathwick, C. and Rigdon, E. (2004) Play, flow, and the online search experience. *Journal of Consumer Research*, 31(2): 324–32.

Morville, P. (2004) User experience design. Retrieved from *http://semanticstudios.com/publications/semantics/ 000029.php*.

Norman, D. (2005) *Emotional Design: Why We Love (or Hate) Everyday Things*. New York: Basic Books.

Norman, D. (2009) *The Design of Future Things*. New York: Basic Books.

Novak, T.P., Hoffman, D.L. and Duhachek, A. (2003) The influence of goal-directed and experiential activities on online flow experiences. *Journal of Consumer Psychology*, 13(1–2): 3–16.

Novak, T.P., Hoffman, D.L. and Yung, Y. (2000) Measuring the customer experience in online environments: A structural modeling approach. *Marketing Science*, 19(1): 22–42.

Palmquist, R. and Kyung-Sun, K. (2000) Cognitive style and on-line database search experience as predictors of websearch performance. *Journal of the American Society for Information Science*, 51(6): 558–66.

Parncutt, R. and McPherson, G.E. (2002) *The Science and Psychology of Music Performance: Creative Strategies for Teaching and Learning Book*. Oxford: Oxford University Press.

Pine, J. and Gilmore, J. (1999) *The Experience Economy: Work is Theater and Every Business a Stage*. Cambridge, MA: Harvard Business Press.

Rathunde, K. and Csikszetimihalyi, M. (2005) Middle school students' motivation and quality of experience: A comparison of Montessori and traditional school environments. *American Journal of Education*, 111(3): 341–71.

Rathunde, K. and Csikszentmihalyi, M. (2006) The developing person: An experiential perspective. In R.M. Lerner and W. Damon (eds.), *Theoretical models of human development, Handbook of child psychology*, 6th edition (pp. 465–515). New York: Wiley.

Rohrer, C. (2008) When to use which user experience research methods. Retrieved from *http://www.useit.com/alertbox/user-research-methods.html*.

Sadeh, T. (2007) Time for a change: new approaches for a new generation of library users. *New Library World*, 108(7/8): 307–16.

Schmidt, A. (2010) New column launch: The user experience. Retrieved from *http://www.libraryjournal.com/article/CA6713142.html*.

Sherry, J. (2004) Flow and media enjoyment. *Communication Theory*, 14(4): 328–47.

Tsai, M. and Tsai, C. (2003) Information searching strategies in web-based science learning: The role of internet self-efficacy. *Innovations in Education and Teaching International*, 40(1): 43–50.

Westerink, J., Ouwerkerk, M., Overbeek, T., Pasveer, W.F. and De Ruyter, B. (eds) (2009) *Probing Experience: From Assessment of User Emotions and Behaviour to Development of Products*. New York: Springer.

Wildemuth. B. (2006) The experience of flow during online searching. Submitted for the ASIST SIG USE 2006 Research Symposium, Information realities: Exploring affective and emotional aspects in information seeking and use. Retrieved from *http://ils.unc.edu/~wildem/ Publications/Flow.SIG USE 2006.pdf*.

6

Narrowing the field: using qualitative approaches to explore specific areas of interest

Abstract: A review of certain topics that are often a challenge for librarians, and how these might become part of a research agenda. The chapter includes discussions of library anxiety, disruptive technology, and the role of the library website.

Key words: library anxiety, disruption, library website, qualitative approaches.

Some library and information service-related challenges are elusive, others have been in the air for a very long time, and librarians and information professionals everywhere have experienced them at some point. This chapter will review a handful of some of the most common, and still pressing, service-related challenges facing librarians, and look at how some researchers have used qualitative approaches to address these concerns.

The library is still scary—a new look at reference by way of an old concept

The use of qualitative data to explore library concerns has been implemented in a variety of libraries—public, academic, special—by numerous researchers. Professionals who interact with users and provide reference help and research support are continually baffled by dwindling numbers of reference questions, despite the fact that there seems to be more information to make sense of. In academic libraries in particular, librarians have sought to discover what holds students in particular back from approaching librarians and asking questions. A brief review of the literature reveals attempts to explore this research question, with numerous articles on library anxiety (Mellon, 1986; Kwon et al., 2007; Onwuegbuzie et al., 2004).

Mellon (1986) used a grounded theory approach to discover the elements of library-related fear. The study revealed the following concepts:

- Students feel that their library use skills are inadequate, as opposed to other students' skills that are adequate.
- This inadequacy is shameful and should be hidden.
- This inadequacy would be revealed by asking questions. (Mellon, 1986, p. 160)

Library anxiety can be defined as "an uncomfortable feeling or emotional disposition, experienced in a library setting, which has cognitive, affective, physiological, and behavioral ramifications" (Jiao et al., 1996, p. 152). In a way, library anxiety very closely mimicked other more well-known types of anxiety, like the type of anxiety that may arise with public speaking, flying, or going into a new work setting for the first time.

Mellon's work (1986) provided a qualitative way to make sense of what students were feeling, and later, another researcher developed a scale to measure levels of library anxiety by way of the Library Anxiety Scale (Bostick, 1992).

This scale has been used extensively by researchers to assess their students' resistance to going to the library, asking for help when they need it, and the impact on their academics (Veal, 2002; Jiao and Onwuegbuzie, 2007; Battle, 2004; Anwar et al., 2004). In fact, Bailey (2008) suggests that "most subsequent research on library anxiety has been based more on Bostick's work than on Mellon's original study" (p. 95). Bostick is best known for articulating five major components of library anxiety: barriers with staff, affective barriers, comfort with the library, knowledge of the library, and mechanical barriers (Onwuegbuzie et al., 2004).

The Mellon study itself is notable for several reasons. First, it used a theory-generating approach to formulate a qualitatively based framework for library anxiety. The data came first, the theory second. Written content generated by the students participating in the study was analyzed for repeating patterns and themes related to their personal research processes, a method called the constant comparative method (Glaser and Strauss, 1967). Eventually, these repeating patterns and themes surfaced Mellon's three theoretical constructs or main ideas—in this case, concepts related to library anxiety. In quantitative studies, the data are used to test pre-existing theory about some phenomena. This marked the first time that a study of this nature used a qualitative approach to document elements related to fear, shame, and unease in a library setting. Finally, it was a large-scale qualitative study (for a library setting).

One of the more interesting phenomena related to the Mellon study was the slew of research that followed (Joseph, 1991; Keefer, 1993; Mech and Brooks, 1997; Shoham and Mizrachi, 2001; Westbrook and DeDecker, 1993; Kracker, 2002; Van Kampen, 2004; Bostick, 1992; Kuhlthau, 1991; Kwon et al., 2007), and the numerous articles by Jiao and Onwuegbuzie (1997a, 1997b, 1999, 2001, 2002). Mellon's work also led to a number of variational studies on the same theme. Researchers have studied graduate students (Jiao and Onwuegbuzie, 1997a); doctoral students (Van Kampen, 2003); foreign students (Anwar et al., 2004; Shoham and Mizrachi, 2001; Abusin and Ngah, 2010); undergraduate students (Kuhlthau, 1988); distance learners (Veal, 2002); at-risk students (Jiao et al., 1996); non-traditional students (Mellon, 1989); and off-campus adult learners (Collins and Veal, 2004). Measures such as the Study Habits Inventory (Jones and Slate, 1992), the Self Perception Profile for College Students (SPPCS), the Computer Anxiety Index, and the Social Interdependence Scale (SIS) have been compared with the Library Anxiety Index to shed light on confounding factors related to anxiety.

What did these various studies reveal about addressing library anxiety, and possible solutions? How did these studies actually impact library services? Jiao and Onwuegbuzie (2002) found that cooperative work and cooperative learning groups "reduced levels of academic-related anxiety for many students" (p. 75). They also found that social interdependence on other students and on librarians plays a significant role in the reduction of library anxiety. The students who rely in a positive manner on others for help tend to be more comfortable using the library, whereas the students who are not cooperatively inclined are less so. One way to address library anxiety in this context is by creating opportunities for students to work in groups and with librarians in a way that is natural and non-threatening, perhaps organized by a course instructor. Librarians embedded in certain lectures may also help to establish their presence as a helpful team member. Onwuegbuzie et al. (2004) suggest three main areas that should be addressed in terms of reducing library anxiety—the physical environment, library instruction, and reference services. As Bailey (2008) points out, these suggestions are not new or earth-shattering; they are, in fact, the same suggestions librarians hear in terms of improving all levels of customer and user service. Nonetheless, the focus on library anxiety provides an interesting perspective from which to view the user experience. Jiao and Onwuegbuzie (1999) further suggest that librarians pay attention to Wine's (1980) cognitive-attentional-interference theory— that is, pay attention to those elements in the environment that increase anxiety and avoidance and decrease focus and positive study behaviors. Librarians are left to decide how this will look in a practical sense, but reducing confusing environmental elements like bad signage, poor web usability, and segmenting library instruction so that sessions are highly subject- or assignment-specific are good places to start.

Jiao and Onwuegbuzie (1999) also examine self-perception, and found that students who are self-perceived as perfectionistic tend to have higher levels of library anxiety. Aspects that focus on psychological and emotional wellbeing of students are normally not the purview of librarians. However, awareness of the relationship between library anxiety and certain psychological elements can only help: "The more [teaching librarians and faculty] know about their students' levels of self-perception, the more effectively they can design and implement measures to help at-risk students to change their psychologically unhealthy and educationally counterproductive self-perceptions and to lead them to academic success" (1999, p. 147). Ansari (2009) found that library anxiety was related to the size of the academic library. Unfortunately, the size of the library is not something that can be easily changed; however, librarians and other teaching professionals can design more welcoming, smaller, and more manageable spaces within pre-existing libraries. Group study spaces, open study enclaves, and reading spaces can all serve to make the library not feel as expansive as it really is.

Library anxiety is not discussed quite as often these days, but the proliferation of technology has created other (real or imagined) challenges for users that impact their behavior when in information seeking and use mode. Chat reference is a good example, with a wide variety of literature published over the past 15 years (Arnold and Kaske, 2005; White et al., 2003; Radford, 2003, 2004a, 2004b; Ronan and Turner, 2002), including qualitative studies (Ward, 2004; Luo, 2007), and related studies about online anxiety (Wang and Chang, 2008). Feeling overwhelmed by too much information, not knowing where to look for expertise, being confused about copyright and plagiarism may all bring about a certain level of anxiety that researchers can continue, and have continued, to explore using qualitative and quantitative data.

Still with us: the library website (The Rutgers Study)

The library website can perhaps be the most useful and the most frustrating information element for both users and those who work in library and information settings. Librarians and others quickly discovered that keeping up with the changing technological environment and having a website that is reflective of what users are used to in their daily lives just is not possible. For many, this means that library websites are often out-of-date, or at least they feel that way. Today, the website is seen by many as nothing more than a gateway to a host of services for the user, whereas, previously, the website in and of itself was the focus. Generation of dynamic content, the creation of my-library suites (personalized services/information on demand), and 24-hour live chat are all ways that libraries have sought to enhance their virtual presence. More recently, libraries are working with mobile technology to reach out to the many users that gain access on-the-go, through their mobile devices. North Carolina State University Libraries Mobile (2010a) was launched in 2009 and allows users to "search for available computers, find hours and locations of branches and library services, look up items in the catalog, and even see the coffee line using the Hill of Beans webcam" (North Carolina State Libraries mobile website, 2010b). MIT (2010) also provides users with mobile access to certain library services, as well as do University of Nebraska Lincoln, Rice University, and the University of Texas. The addition of mobile-enabled content does create a number of additional considerations for those working with library web designs. The library website remains the main source of communication with the user. Qualitative approaches can help librarians and others to determine what services and improvements are going to be most beneficial. And even for the old-fashioned website, these approaches can provide a refreshing and novel look at the user. The following is an example of how qualitative methods informed the redesign process for a university library's website.

Starting in January 2009, the Rutgers University Libraries began the process of reconceptualizing the library website. The website had been through various iterations and, like many library websites, felt cluttered and confusing. Website redesign can go one of two ways—either an outside design firm is brought in to redo the site, or internal staff is commissioned to lead the charge. After investigating a number of large commercial firms, the staff at Rutgers decided that a more personalized and user-driven approach to the redesign might be best. An anthropologist was brought in to lead what would become an ethnographic study of the library's website and its users. Specifically, the study examined how graduates, undergraduates, and faculty used the website to access information and conduct research, and how the website helped them to integrate the library into their work. The role of the anthropologist was to inform the library team about the ethnographic process, its design, inputs, and outputs. Since conducting an ethnographic study was very different than just doing a usability study, the process was new to many of the librarians and staff involved. The end goal was to amass a rich collection of data about users that could not be gotten through just a questionnaire or observation session alone. These data would then need to be analyzed, examined for patterns, then somehow used to interpret user needs—all with the end goal of designing a more useful website, keeping the current users and attracting new users.

Gathering the data for the Rutgers study involved two strategies—conducting a survey and extended in-person interviews with participants. These two approaches, one of which produced quantitative data and the other qualitative data, were combined during the project's findings phase. Core and project teams consisting of library faculty and staff directed the study, with the visiting anthropologist taking the lead.

A total of 6,390 graduate and undergraduate students completed the initial survey. The survey respondents covered a variety of disciplines, with 1,395 (21.8 percent) from the arts and humanities, 497 (7.77 percent) from business, 1,952 (30.51 percent) from the social sciences, and 2,546 (39.79 percent) from the sciences, technology, engineering, and medicine (STEM).

For the qualitative portion of the study, 21 undergraduate students and eight graduate students participated in semi-structured interviews.

The result was an 82-page ethnography (White, 2009), which describes in great detail the work and research habits of the students. The interview questions focused on the culture of research, student habits, and website use as they related to general site navigation, issues of design and efficacy, problems with vendor-related content and links, federated searching, interaction with librarians, the use of bibliographic management software (RefWorks, Zotero, etc.), and social networking (White, 2009).

Each interview took anywhere from 40 to 60 minutes. The interviews were videorecorded, and conducted by the lead anthropologist. Each videotaped session was then viewed by various members of the project team, and during these "coviewing" sessions team members were able to discuss informally their observations and thoughts about the information from the interview. The interviews were each transcribed by an independent transcription company, which produced more than 800 pages of raw text. The lead anthropologist then used a software program (HyperResearch) to facilitate the coding of the data. It was this coding that allowed for the various repeating ideas and themes to be revealed.

The findings from the study ran the gamut from the expected to the shocking. One of the more interesting findings was that "website users do not want to read and be instructed, except perhaps by choice" (White, 2009). The study also revealed that users wanted a tool, not just a "vehicle for library information" (White, 2009). In other words, providing access and acting as a gateway were no longer enough. In the end, the Rutgers team established seven redesign principles and a corresponding list of priorities to guide the actual redesign of the website: flexibility, integrations, information literacy, simplicity, context, self-sufficiency, and process (White, 2009). The general priorities were to make access easier, make finding e-journals simpler, improve navigation, surface high-demand resources, match user expectation in Web 2.0 in color layout, widgets, and services, improve personalization and context, simplify design elements, fix what's broken, and improve the top page (White, 2009).

The Rutgers Libraries website is still being redesigned according to the study's findings. The decision to gather qualitative data and compile an ethnography of the culture of student research allowed the Rutgers team to develop greater insight into the research habits and needs of the users. From the beginning, the study focused almost exclusively on the user, as opposed to the traditional process of website redesign where the site itself is the focus. The ethnography remains a very powerful tool for understanding today's user, especially when combined with quantitative data, which can be analyzed inferentially. The novelty in the ethnographic approach is primarily evidenced by the creation of the ethnography, the "thick description" (Geertz, 1973), which provided a way to understand the culture of research within the academic context. Repeating ideas gave way to themes that were then examined for their relationship to the redesign of the website. The themes related to the website and its use came directly from interaction and discussion with the users, so the users themselves generated these ideas.

Disruption and the information seeker

These days, information service providers, media outlets, merchants, and educators want to know more about the digital habits of users from all age groups. As discussed in Chapter 4 of this book, there is great interest in the habits of young people born between 1980 and 1994, but the interest does not end there. Mobile and wireless technologies will continue to disrupt the way information services are provided in a variety of settings. Disruptive technologies include those that cause a "major change in 'the accepted way of doing things', including business models, processes, revenue streams, industry dynamics and consumer behaviour" (Gartner Group, 2010). The initial definition of disruptive technology was coined by Bower and Christensen (1995), who define such technologies as those that can render the surrounding industries and organizations obsolete by presenting unanticipated technological changes and the subsequent impact. The Gartner Group, an international information technology research firm, defines the most disruptive technologies for 2008–10 as follows:

- Multicore and hybrid processors
- Virtualisation and fabric computing
- Social networks and social software
- Cloud computing and cloud/web platforms
- Web mashups
- User interface
- Ubiquitous computing
- Contextual computing
- Augmented reality
- Semantics. (Gartner Group, 2010)

From a library point of view, there are several technologies on this list that are already having an impact on the way services are provided, including cloud computing, user interfaces, and social networks. In fact, none of the items on the list are a surprise, nor are they that new. They were at the time of their creation and continue to be disruptive because, in many cases, those of us in library settings were not able to adequately anticipate their impact on us as professionals, or on our users. Lafferty and Edwards (2004) state that the academic library faces some of the same challenges presented by disruption as do commercial entities. "It should come as no surprise if at some time in the future, the university disappears in the face of disruption. However, it may be that institutions survive and only their libraries disappear" (Lafferty and Edwards, 2004, p. 255). The authors suggest that higher education itself, scholarly publishing, and the academic library are already at risk. While some researchers suggest that the disruption has already happened (Hawkins, 2001), those of us who work in library settings recognize that the disruption is a slow progression that is hard to predict, and that it is very much still happening.

How have researchers examined the impact of disruptive and other technology, and what can libraries learn from these research efforts? There are some intriguing examples. Jones et al. (2004) examined the relationship between geographic space and people's social, communication, and information interactions, to "clarify the role of place information in social interaction" (p. 202), with the end goal of designing a place-aware community system, to "incorporate the concept of physical places into systems" (p. 202). Modern-day disruptive technologies like wireless, RFID, and GPS now allow for people, places, and information to be connected (p. 203), but relevance and meaning are not always factored in. The researchers used qualitative methods "to explore people's actual personal experiences of place, everyday activities, and associated information needs" (Jones et al., 2004, p. 204). Participants kept a place diary, and participated in semi-structured interviews. The study revealed some interesting findings, which in some cases may be relevant to libraries:

- While informants did identify information needs based on place-types, place was not the sole factor; rather, needs were primarily based on the *activity* taking place.

- A key factor in determining whether and what type of information people needed was how *frequently* they performed a particular activity in a place.

- Whether information was relatively *stable* or *dynamic* also influenced people's needs. Stable information includes things like train schedules and restaurant menus; dynamic information includes things such as whether a particular train is running late and the waiting time to be seated at a restaurant.

- There were interactions between these factors: for example, if people engaged in a particular activity in a place frequently, they had little need in obtaining stable information, but judged dynamic information to be useful. (Jones et al., 2004, p. 205)

Libraries encounter a wide variety of users, each engaged in different activities relative to where they are physically or virtually. Some users have very rigid patterns of use and habits, and utilize the same resources over and over again. Other users are open to the power of serendipity, and browse/ search for information in a less structured way. Users may (or may not) fit into the following information/activity pairings described by the authors:

- *Stable Information/Frequent Activity*—Users engage in an activity in a specific place frequently to get activity-related information that does not change over time.

- *Stable Information/Infrequent Activity*—Although the activity-related information is stable, the users' activity is infrequent.

- *Dynamic Information/Frequent Activities*—Users require frequent updates of information related to activities that they do often, because the information itself changes constantly (a good example might be a graduate student who reviews weekly the table of contents from the major journals in their field).

- *Dynamic Information/Infrequent Activities*—Users require updates of dynamic information related to activities that they do not do often. (Jones et al., 2004, p. 205)

The researchers concluded that the location or type of information alone does not determine information needs; rather, it is the relationship between "user routines" and "social relationships" (Jones et al., 2004, p. 210).

The impact of place-aware technology such as GPS and RFID has been discussed and some programs even implemented in a number of public and academic libraries (Shahid, 2005; Erwin and Kern, 2003; Kern, 2004; Choi et al., 2006; Golding and Tennant, 2007). However, the literature tends to focus much more on the technology rather than on the user. One research approach might therefore be to learn more about the social implications of place-aware technology on research practices, resource use, and teaching. In the academic library, this can be even more relevant if there is a broader interest on the campus about integrating place-aware technology with distance learning, mobile technologies, and learning management systems such as Blackboard and Sakai.

In another study aimed at understanding the impact of disruptive technologies on users, Brown et al. (2000) used participant diaries to learn more about how people capture information—whether the information consists of photographic images, movies, or notes on paper. Their analysis of 22 user diaries helped them to construct a design and analysis taxonomy (p. 438). The researchers justified their project by citing the lack of literature on the topic, despite a growing need to understand how users capture information in everyday life, particularly in the workplace. Fast-forward to 2011, and think about the various reasons that a library user needs to capture information.

It is not unusual to find college students who, when faced with the fact that they cannot download the entirety of an article for whatever reasons, take a screenshot of the available pages with a cell phone or PDA for later reference. The same is true for images and photographs found in books and reserves materials—as opposed to making a photocopy, or checking out a book, students take a picture with whatever technology they have available and refer to that image when need be. This type of information capture is relatively common (Doermann et al., 2003; Barreau et al., 2006), and the technology to increase resolution, sharing, and ease of use is always being improved, yet little can be found in the library and information services literature about these practices as they relate to information gathering. Certainly, learning more about these capture practices, by way of user diaries, unobtrusive methods, participant observation, and semi-structured interviews might be very enlightening for librarians.

So far, this book has explored qualitative research activities as they relate to library and information service users. The next chapter takes a slightly different approach, and examines the potential for workplace research on the library, with a focus on the people who work there.

References

Abusin, K.A. and Ngah, Z.A. (2010) Exploring library anxiety among Sudanese university students. *Malaysian Journal of Library and Information Science*, 15(1): 55–81.

Ansari, N. (2009) The relationship between perceived size of library collection and library anxiety among undergraduate students at International Islamic University Malaysia. *Proceedings of ICAL 2009—Management Models and Framework.* Retrieved from *http://crl.du.ac.in/ical09/papers/index_files/ical-72_34_160_2_RV.pdf.*

Anwar, M.A., Al-Kandari, N.M. and Al-Qallaf, C. (2004) Use of Bostick's library anxiety scale on undergraduate biological sciences students of Kuwait University. *Library and Information Science Research*, 26: 266–83.

Arnold, J. and Kaske, N. (2005) Evaluating the quality of a chat service. *Libraries and the Academy*, 5(2): 177–93.

Bailey, E. (2008) Constance Mellon demonstrated that college freshmen are afraid of academic libraries. A review of: Mellon, Constance A. "Library anxiety: A grounded theory and its development." *Evidence Based Library and Information Practice*, 3(3): 94–7.

Barreau, D., Crystal, A., Greenberg, J., Sharma, A., Conway, M., Oberlin, J., Shoffner, M. and Seiberling, S. (2006) Augmenting memory for student learning: Designing a context-aware capture system for biology education. *Proceedings of the American Society for Information Science and Technology*, 43(1): 1–6.

Battle, J.C. (2004) The effect of information literacy instruction on library anxiety among international students. Unpublished dissertation, University of North Texas.

Bostick, S.L. (1992) The development and validation of the library anxiety scale. Unpublished doctoral dissertation, Wayne State University School of Information and Library Studies.

Bower, J.L. and Christensen, C.M. (1995) Disruptive technologies: Catching the wave. *Harvard Business Review*, January–February: 43–52.

Brown, B., Sellen, A. and O'Hara, K. (2000) A diary study of information capture in working life. *Proceedings of CHI 2000, Conference on Human Factors in Computing Systems*, The Hague, 438–45.

Choi, J.W., Oh, D. and Song, I. (2006) R-LIM: an affordable library search system based on RFID. *Proceedings of the 2006 International Conference on Hybrid Information Technology*, 1: 103–8.

Collins, K.M.T. and Veal, R. (2004) Off-campus adult learners' levels of library anxiety as a predictor of attitudes towards the internet. *Library and Information Research*, 26(1): 5–14.

Doermann, D., Liang, J. and Li, H. (2003) Progress in camera-based document image analysis. *Proceedings of the Seventh International Conference on Document Analysis and Recognition (ICDAR)*, 1: 606.

Erwin, E. and Kern, C. (2003) Radio-frequency-identification for security and media circulation in libraries. *Library and Archival Security*, 18(2): 23–38.

The Gartner Group (2010) Retrieved from *http://www .gartner.com/it/page.jsp?id=681107#_ftn1*.

Geertz, C. (1973) Thick description: Toward an interpretive theory of culture. In *The Interpretation of Cultures: Selected Essays*. New York: Basic Books.

Glaser, B.G. and Strauss, A.L. (1967) *The Discovery of Grounded Theory: Strategies for Qualitative Research*. Chicago, IL: Aldine Publishing Company.

Golding, P. and Tennant, V. (2007) Work in progress: Performance and reliability of radio frequency identification (RFID) library system. 2007 International Conference on Multimedia and Ubiquitous Engineering (MUE'07). Retrieved from *http://www.computer.org/ portal/web/csdl/doi/10.1109/MUE.2007.219*.

Hawkins, B.L. (2001) Information access in the digital era: Challenges and a call for collaboration. *EDUCAUSE Review*, 36(5): 50–7.

Jiao, Q. and Onwuegbuzie, A. (1997a) Perfectionism and library anxiety among graduate students. *Journal of Academic Librarianship*, 24(5): 365–71.

Jiao, Q. and Onwuegbuzie, A. (1997b) The antecedents of library anxiety. *Library Quarterly*, 67: 372–89.

Jiao, Q. and Onwuegbuzie, A. (1999) Self-perception and library anxiety: An empirical study. *Library Review*, 48(3): 140–7.

Jiao, Q. and Onwuegbuzie, A. (2001) Library anxiety and characteristic strengths and weaknesses of graduate students' study habits. *Library Review*, 50(2): 73–80.

Jiao, Q. and Onwuegbuzie, A. (2002) Dimensions of library anxiety and social interdependence: implications for library services. *Library Review*, 51(2): 71–8.

Jiao, Q., Onwuegbuzie, A. and Lichtenstein, A. (1996) Library anxiety: Characteristics of "at-risk" college students. *Library and Information Science Research*, 18: 151–63.

Jones, C.H. and Slate, J.R. (1992) Technical manual for the study habits inventory. Unpublished manuscript, Arkansas State University, Jonesboro, AR.

Jones, Q., et al. (2004) Putting systems into place: A qualitative study of design requirements for location-aware community systems. *Proceedings of the 2004 ACM Conference on Computer Supported Cooperative Work*, 202–111.

Joseph, M.E. (1991) The cure for library anxiety: It may not be what you think. *Catholic Library World*, 63: 111–14.

Keefer, J. (1993) The hungry rats syndrome: Library anxiety, information literacy, and the academic reference process. *RQ*, 32: 333–9.

Kern, C. (2004) Radio-frequency-identification for security and media circulation in libraries. *Electronic Library*, 22(4): 317–24.

Kracker, J. (2002) Research anxiety and students' perceptions of research: An experiment. Part I. Effect of teaching Kuhlthau's ISP model. *Journal of the American Society for Information Science and Technology*, 53(4): 282–94.

Kuhlthau, C. (1988) Longitudinal case studies of the information search process of users in libraries. *Library and Information Science Research*, 10(3): 257–304.

Kuhlthau, C. (1991) Inside the search process: Information seeking from the user's perspective. *Journal of the American Society for Information Science*, 42(5): 361–71.

Kwon, N., Onwuegbuzie, A. and Alexander, L. (2007) Critical thinking disposition and library anxiety: Affective domains on the space of information seeking and use in academic libraries. *College and Research Libraries*, 68(3): 268–78.

Lafferty, S. and Edwards, J. (2004) Disruptive technologies: What future universities and their libraries? *Library Management*, 25 (6/7): 252–8.

Luo, L. (2007) Chat reference competencies: Identification from a literature review and librarian interviews. *Reference Services Review*, 35(2): 195–209.

Mech, T.F. and Brooks, C.I. (1997) Anxiety and confidence in using a library by college freshmen and seniors. *Psychological Reports*, 81: 929–30.

Mellon, C. (1989) Library anxiety and the non-traditional student. In T. Mensching (ed.), *Reaching and teaching diverse library user groups* (pp. 77–81). Ann Arbor, MI: Pierian Press.

Mellon, C. (1986) Library anxiety: A grounded theory and its development, *College and Research Libraries*, 47(2): 160–5.

MIT Libraries Mobile (2010) *http://libraries.mit.edu/mobile-site/*.

North Carolina State University Libraries Mobile (2010a) *http://www.lib.ncsu.edu/dli/projects/librariesmobile/*.

North Carolina State University Libraries Mobile (2010b) *http://www.lib.ncsu.edu/m/about.html*.

Onwuegbuzie, A., Jiao, Q. and Bostick, S. (2004) *Library Anxiety: Theory, Research, and Applications*. Los Angeles, CA: Scarecrow Press.

Radford, M. (2003) In synch? Evaluating chat reference transcripts. Virtual Reference Desk: 5th Annual Digital Reference Conference. Retrieved from *www.webjunction.org/do/DisplayContent/jsessionid=F3D25772218194BEB7652D4CFD1AE98F?id=12664*.

Radford, M. (2004a) Hmmm . . . Just a moment while I keep looking: Interpersonal communication in chat reference. RUSA 10th Annual Reference Research Forum. Retrieved from *www.ala.org/ala/rusa/rusaourassoc/rusasections/rss/rsssection/rsscomm/rssresstat/2004refreschfrm.cfm*.

Radford, M. (2004b) Yo dude! YRU typin so slow? Virtual reference desk: 6th Annual Digital Reference Conference. Retrieved from *www.webjunction.org/do/DisplayContent?id=12497*.

Ronan, J. and Turner, C. (2002) *Chat Reference*. Washington, DC: Association of Research Libraries.

Shahid, S. (2005) Use of RFID technology in libraries: a new approach to circulation, tracking, inventorying, and security of library materials. *Library Philosophy and Practice*, 8, 1–9.

Shoham, S. and Mizrachi, D. (2001) Library anxiety among undergraduates: A study of Israeli B.Ed. students. *Journal of Academic Librarianship*, 27(4): 305–11.

Van Kampen, D. (2004) Development and validation of the multidimensional library anxiety scale. *College and Research Libraries*, 65(1): 28–34.

Van Kampen, D. (2003) *Library Anxiety, the Information Search Process, and Doctoral Students' Use of the Library.* Orlando: University of Central Florida.

Veal, R. (2002) The relationship between library anxiety and off-campus adult learners. *Journal of Library Administration*, 37(33): 529–36.

Ward, D. (2004) Measuring the completeness of reference transactions in online chats: Results of an unobtrusive study. *Reference and User Services Quarterly*, 44(1): 46–56.

Wang, C. and Chang, S. (2008) Online chat dependency: The influence of social anxiety. *IEIC—Transactions on Information and Systems*, E91-D(6): 1622–7.

Westbrook, L. and DeDecker, S. (1993) Supporting user needs and skills to minimize library anxiety. *Reference Librarian*, 40: 43–51.

White, C.T. (2009) Studying students: The ethnographic research project at Rutgers University. Retrieved from *http://www.libraries.rutgers.edu/rul/staff/groups/ethnography/reports/ERP_FinalReport_Phase_1.pdf.*

White, M.D., Abels, E.G. and Kaske, N. (2003) Evaluation of chat reference service quality. *D-Lib Magazine*, 9(2). Retrieved from *www.dlib.org/dlib/february03/white/02white.html.*

Wine, J. (1980) Cognitive-attentional theory of test anxiety. In I.G. Sarason (ed.), *Test anxiety: Theory, research and applications*, (pp. 349–385). Hillsdale, NJ: Erlbaum.

7

What about us? Using qualitative methods to explore the library as workplace

Abstract: This chapter explores how qualitative workplace research can inform service and practice within library settings. Ethnographic workplace studies from other environments are discussed.

Key words: workplace research, qualitative interviews, technology adoption, ethnographic approach.

Various strategies to study and hopefully improve library and information services and settings for users by applying qualitative approaches have so far been discussed at length in this book. In every library and information setting, the staff are an integral part of the enterprise, and this chapter will explore ways in which qualitative approaches might be used to learn more about the environments that librarians work in, their work practices, interaction and collaboration structures, and beliefs and attitudes, in their natural environments.

Researchers in a variety of areas have used qualitative approaches to learn more about employees in the workplace. This is particularly true in the health sciences (Nilsson et al., 2005; Ivarsson and Nilsson, 2009). Work environments such as adult entertainment (Grandy, 2008; Lian et al., 2000;

Bruckert, 2002); day labor (Ahonen et al., 2009); social work (Chanmugam, 2009); and psychology (Sturgeon and Morrissette, 2010) have also been studied. Researchers have even studied the impact of the qualitative interview itself on workers' job performance (Butterfield et al., 2009). Workplace ethnographies are commonly found in the anthropological and sociological literature, including titles such as *Royal Blue, the Culture of Construction Workers* (Applebaum, 1981); *Team Toyota: Transplanting the Toyota Culture to the Camry Plant in Kentucky* (Besser, 1996); *The Scalpel's Edge: The Culture of Surgeons* (Katz, 1998); and *Inside Nursing: A Critical Ethnography of Clinical Nursing Practice* (Street, 1992).

The use and adoption of workplace technology are another area that has been extensively explored, in many cases using qualitative approaches. For instance, Bradner et al. (1999) explored the use of chat in the workplace; and Stiroh (2008) and Bartel et al. (2007) examined the impact of technology on productivity. Examples of qualitative studies of the library/ information service workplace and profession are not as numerous. Stover (2000) collected qualitative survey data from librarians about their attitudes regarding the impact of the Internet. Montiel-Overall (2008) looked at librarian-teacher collaboration within the context of a qualitative study, and Boon (2006) studied the female experience of librarians at small community libraries using case studies and categorical analysis. Shachak et al. (2007) explored medical librarians' adoption of bioinformatics tools using exploratory interviews and content analysis of the data; and Ameen (2008) explored book acquisition in Pakistan and coded interview data using categorical analysis. Walter (2006, 2008) explored the professional identity of librarians, and Marshall et al. (2009) used qualitative methods to examine what factors influence librarians' professional career choices.

What are some of the reasons for studying the internal working world and workplace culture of librarianship and libraries? Hodson (2004) suggests that workplace ethnographies, for instance, can reveal the "effects of organizational characteristics on employee attitudes and behaviors" (p. 4). It may sound like somewhat of an indulgence—there is barely enough time to conduct user-focused research, let alone research that is introspective, in most library settings. However, developing a better understanding of work practice, interaction and collaboration patterns, beliefs and attitudes may actually help librarians and those working in libraries to be more effective. Workplace research is conducted for a variety of reasons. Randall and Rouncefield (2000) suggest that the "analysis of work" involves the investigation of socially organized human activities and the patterns of interaction and collaboration. Evaluating the emotional and psychological impacts of any given job can be key in terms of discovering and alleviating factors that interfere with productivity. A good example is the ethnography *Juggling Food and Feelings: Emotional Balance in the Workplace* (Gatta, 2002), where the author explored the emotional landscape of women in the restaurant industry. Employees who work in high-stress environments, such as air traffic controllers and surgeons, tend to suffer higher rates of burnout and mind-body illnesses, and these populations have been the subject of myriad ethnographic workplace studies as well (Baker, 1985; Cooper et al., 1986; Grandjean et al., 1971). The findings from qualitative workplace studies may help improve the motivation, productivity, health, and wellbeing of workers. These studies may also help gauge readiness for and reactions to organizational change (Cunningham et al., 2002).

Adoption of technology (Morris and Venkatesh, 2000) by workers is an area that has a lot of research appeal, especially given the role of technology in society. Researchers have used case studies, field studies, and diary studies to explore technology adoption in elderly populations (Selwyn, 2004), health care workers (Lu et al., 2005), and millennials (Grinter and Palen, 2002). This topic might be particularly relevant in library and information settings (Rabina and Walczyk, 2007; Ramzan, 2004; Kahan, 1997), although the literature reveals few studies, qualitative or otherwise. "Research regarding adoption, rejection, and dissonance of technology by librarians is scarce. Much of the research regarding innovativeness and diffusion of library technology has focused on library patrons such as faculty or students" (Rabina and Walczyk, 2007). Librarians' adoption of technology can impact instruction, reference, and administrative activities. Qualitative studies might be structured to capture different aspects of technology adoption. Video diaries might be used to document librarians' adoption of new instructional technology such as Moodle or Sakai. Diaries might explore their experiences with new repository technology, and qualitative interviews might be used to find out more about library administrators' decision-making processes in times of technological transition.

A trend or development that has been examined on an exploratory level in the literature is a good candidate for further qualitative study, assuming the topic is relevant for a particular library. For instance, Burnette and Dorsch (2006), Peters et al. (2003), Scollin et al. (2006), Shipman and Morton (2001), and Smith (2002) discuss the widespread use of PDAs by librarians in medical libraries. However, none of these studies made use of collected qualitative data to better understand the phenomenon. Certainly, in environments where librarians and library staff continue to use PDAs for work-related activities, and increasingly devices such as the iPad and iPhone, learning more about the impact on collaboration, interaction patterns, and daily activity in the librarians' natural environment might be eye-opening. These are just a few examples of areas of interest found in the literature. Librarians will have to judge for themselves which topics are relevant and meaningful to their own work environments.

References

Ahonen, E.Q., Porthé, V., Vázquez, M.L., García,, A.M., López-Jacob, M.J., Ruiz-Frutos, C., Ronda-Pérez, E., Benach, J. and Benavides, F.G. (2009) A qualitative study about immigrant workers' perceptions of their working conditions in Spain. *Journal of Epidemiological Community Health*, 63(11): 936–42.

Ameen, K. (2008) Perceptions and self-assessment of university librarians regarding Collection Management (CM): A case study of Pakistan. *Collection Building*, 27(4): 167–73.

Applebaum, H. (1981) *Royal Blue, the Culture of Construction Workers*. New York: Holt Rinehart & Winston.

Baker, D. (1985) The study of stress at work. *Annual Review of Public Health*, 6, 367–81.

Bartel, A., Ichniowski, C. and Shaw, K. (2007) How does information technology affect productivity? Plant-level comparisons of product innovation, process improvement, and worker skills. *Quarterly Journal of Economics*, 122(4): 1721–58.

Besser, T. (1996) *Team Toyota: Transplanting the Toyota Culture to the Camry Plant in Kentucky*. Albany, NY: State University of New York Press.

Boon, B. (2006) The professional development of small community librarians in Texas: A qualitative study of the female experience. Unpublished doctoral dissertation, University of Texas at Austin.

Bradner, E., Kellogg, W.A. and Erickson, T. (1999) The adoption and use of babble: A field study of chat in the workplace. *Proceedings of the Sixth European Conference on Computer Supported Cooperative Work*, Copenhagen, 139–58. Retrieved from *http://portal.acm.org/citation.cfm?id=351698*.

Bruckert, C. (2002) *Taking It Off, Putting It On: Women Working in Strip Clubs*. Toronto, CA: Canadian Scholar's Press.

Burnette, P. and Dorsch, J. (2006) From novelty to necessity: Impact of the PDA experience on medical libraries. *Reference Librarian*, 45(93): 83–98.

Butterfield, L., Borgen, W. and Amundson, N.E. (2009) The impact of a qualitative research interview on workers' views of their situation. *Canadian Journal of Counselling/ Revue canadienne de counseling*, 43(2): 120–30.

Chanmugam, A. (2009) A qualitative study of school social workers' clinical and professional relationships when reporting child maltreatment. *Children and Schools*, 31(3): 145–61.

Cooper, C., Lawson, G. and Price, V. (1986) A survey of stress at work. *Occupational Medicine*, 36(2): 71–2.

Cunningham, C.E., Woodward, C.A., Shannon, H.S., MacIntosh, J., Lendrum, B., Rosenbloom, D. and Brown, J. (2002) Readiness for organizational change: A longitudinal study of workplace, psychological and behavioural correlates. *Journal of Occupational and Organizational Psychology*, 75(4): 377–92.

Gatta, M. (2002) *Juggling Food and Feelings: Emotional Balance in the Workplace*. Lanham, MD: Lexington Books.

Grandjean, E.P., Wotzka, G., Schaad, R. and Gilgen, A. (1971) Fatigue and stress in air traffic controllers. *Ergonomics*, 14(1): 159–65.

Grandy, G. (2008) Managing spoiled identities: Dirty workers' struggles for a favourable sense of self. *Qualitative Research in Organizations and Management: An International Journal*, 3(3): 176–98.

Grinter, R. and Palen, L. (2002) Instant messaging in teen life. *Proceedings of the 2002 ACM Conference on Computer-Supported Work*, New Orleans, LA. Retrieved from *http://www.cs.colorado.edu/~palen/Papers/grinter-palen-IM.pdf*.

Hodson, R. (2004) A meta-analysis of workplace ethnographies: Race, gender, and employee attitudes and behaviors. *Journal of Contemporary Ethnography*, 33(1): 4–38.

Ivarsson, B. and Nilsson, G. (2009) The subject of pedagogy from theory to practice—the view of newly registered nurses. *Nurse Education Today*, 29(5): 510–15.

Kahan, R. (1997) Attitudes of East Tennessee medical librarians about evolving computer information technology. *Tennessee Librarian*, 49(1): 19–26.

Katz, P. (1998) *The Scalpel's Edge: The Culture of Surgeons*. New York: Allyn & Bacon.

Lian, W.M., Chan, R. and Wee, S. (2000) Sex workers' perspectives on condom use for oral sex with clients: A qualitative study. *Health Education Behavior*, 27(4): 502–16.

Lu, Y., Xiao, Y., Sears, A. and Jacko, J.A. (2005) A review and a framework of handheld computer adoption in healthcare. *International Journal of Medical Informatics*, 74(5): 409–22.

Marshall, V., Rathbun-Grubb, S. and Marshall, J.G. (2009) Using the life course perspective to study library and information science careers. *Library Trends*, 58(2): 127–40.

Montiel-Overall, P. (2008) Teacher and librarian collaboration: A qualitative study. *Library and Information Science Research*, 30(2): 145–55.

Morris, M. and Venkatesh, V. (2000) Age differences in technology adoption decisions: Implications for a changing work force. *Personnel Psychology*, 53(2): 375–403.

Nilsson, K., Hertting, A., Petterson, I. and Theorell, T. (2005) Pride and confidence at work: Potential predictors of occupational health in a hospital setting. *BMC Public Health*, 5: 92.

Peters, T.A., Dorsch, J., Bell, L. and Burnette, P. (2003) PDAs and the health science libraries. *Library Hi Tech*, 21(4): 400–11.

Rabina, D. and Walczyk, D. (2007) Information professionals' attitude toward the adoption of innovations in everyday life. *Information Research*, 12(4). Retrieved from *http://informationr.net/ir/12-4/colis/colis12.html*.

Ramzan, M. (2004) Effects of IT utilization and knowledge on librarians' IT attitudes. *Electronic Library*, 22(5): 440–7.

Randall, D. and Rouncefield, M. (2000) The theory and practice of fieldwork for Systems Development. Retrieved from *http://www.comp.lancs.ac.uk/sociology/Fieldwork/Tutout.html*.

Scollin, P., Callahan, J., Mehta, A. and Garcia, E. (2006) The PDA as a reference tool: libraries' role in enhancing nursing education. *Computers Informatics Nursing*, 24(4): 208–13.

Selwyn, N. (2004) The information aged: A qualitative study of older adults' use of information and communications technology. *Journal of Aging Studies*, 18(4): 369–84.

Shachak, A., Shuval, K. and Fine, S. (2007) Barriers and enablers to the acceptance of bioinformatics tools: A qualitative study. *Journal of the Medical Library Association*, 95(4): 454–8.

Shipman, J.P. and Morton, A.C. (2001) The new black bag: PDAs, health care and library services. *Reference Services Review*, 29(3): 229–38.

Smith, R. (2002) Adapting a new technology to the academic medical library: Personal digital assistants. *Journal of the Medical Library Association*, 90(1): 93–4.

Stiroh, K. (2008) Information technology and productivity: Old answers and new questions. *CESifo Economic Studies*, 54(3): 358–85.

Stover, M. (2000) Reference librarians and the internet: A qualitative study. *Reference Service Review*, 28(1): 39–46.

Street, A. (1992) *Inside Nursing: A Critical Ethnography of Clinical Nursing Practice*. Albany, NY: State University of New York Press.

Sturgeon, R. and Morrissette, P. (2010) A qualitative analysis of suicide ideation among Manitoban farmers. *Canadian Journal of Counselling/Revue canadienne de counseling*, 44(2): 191–207.

Walter, S. (2006) Instructional improvement: Building capacity for the professional development of librarians as teachers. *Reference and User Services Quarterly*, 45(3): 213–18.

Walter, S. (2008) Librarians as teachers: A qualitative inquiry into professional identity. *College and Research Libraries*, 69(1): 51–71.

8

A place in the world: qualitative research as a way to study global libraries

Abstract: This chapter explores a novel project, located in rural Uganda, which used qualitative methods to explore communication exchange amongst rural village library users.

Key words: Uganda, Africa, village libraries, storytelling, grounded theory, narrative analysis, content analysis.

So far, this book has focused exclusively on qualitative research in the modern Western library setting. Many aspects of daily life are now impacted on some level by globalism, whether it be business, technology, or education. Libraries are no exception; they operate in all corners of the developed and still-developing world, and librarians and library professionals provide services for a wide variety of users of many different languages, backgrounds, and cultures. Qualitative research in these settings can focus on the needs of users, the use of technology, and collection development, to name a few. In libraries that operate in the developing world, qualitative research can take on a very rich meaning; it can also reveal cultural and social patterns of interaction, social and cultural norms and beliefs, and information about communication, values, and societal structures.

This chapter will present one example of qualitative research used to study certain phenomena related to a rural African village library in Uganda. Specifically, this study utilizes a qualitative content analysis approach to explore information transfer in the way of stories told by library users (mothers/grandmothers to their children). The aim of the study is to discover then understand any patterns, themes, and theoretical constructs within these narratives related to the library within the sociocultural context of life in this rural Ugandan village. Since the study is exploratory in nature, it aims to generate, rather than test, research questions about the nature of these mothers'/grandmothers' stories, which may in turn be used to guide future examination of theoretical constructs. This is often the case with qualitative research of this type.

This example is intended to highlight the diversity of qualitative approaches and the ways in which it can work in traditional library settings and in library-related settings that may be more typical of anthropological field studies.

Why use a qualitative approach?

This project is based on research conducted during the summer of 2009 in the rural Ugandan villages of Kitengesa and Gulema. It represents part of a larger constellation of studies (Dent and Yannotta, 2005; Dent, 2006a, 2006b, 2007; Dent Goodman, 2008; Parry, 2004) which have investigated the impact of rural village libraries in Uganda and elsewhere in Africa on the users they serve, using both qualitative and quantitative data. The 2009 intergenerational study focused on the learning-readiness of young children (5 to 7 years old) as influenced by the reading habits of their primary caregivers—in this case, their mothers/grandmothers. The project included more than 100 hours spent interviewing 51 caregivers about their reading and literary practices, their home lives, and their health and socioeconomic status.

This particular project used a qualitative approach because of the type of data to be examined (stories), but also because of the cultural framework in which the study took place. Identifying cultural information transfer in a culture that still struggles with high rates of illiteracy presents certain challenges, especially when current research trends tend to focus solely on information and knowledge transfer as products of literacy. Traditional oral practices are often not integrated into efforts to increase literacy, yet, in many cultures worldwide, orality remains one of the major modes of communication (Ong, 2002). Studying narratives and stories has long been an approach used by researchers to learn more about cultures, organizations, individuals, and events. In this case, examining these stories is a way to highlight their continued relevance and importance to those who shared them, the tellers and the listeners. Anyone who has listened to traditional tales, old proverbs, or original stories can attest to the fact that they are incredibly rich, creative, and often complex, bearing multiple meanings for both those who tell them, and those who hear them. The researchers of the study share a profound respect for the importance of this kind of oral transmission, no matter what the cultural backdrop is. At the same time, a better understanding of the inherent meaning, themes, and impact of these stories within a research context may be able to support an increased awareness of their continued role within both oral and literate cultures. This may ensure that research, whether on literacy, rural village libraries, or language development, remains respectful and inclusive of these practices.

An ethnographic study of this type encompasses more than just the phenomena being studied; thus this study and its outcomes were reviewed within the context of what it means to live in Uganda in this day and age. Impediments to wellbeing and health are always present, and include disease (especially malaria and HIV); famine; threats to hygiene; lack of access to clean water; low educational attainment; low literacy rates; and even more sinister dangers, such as kidnapping, ritualistic murder and sacrifice, and familial violence. One of the key goals of the original Ugandan rural village library study was to gather empirical evidence on the positive impact of these libraries, in order to support those in other rural areas of Uganda (and other parts of Africa) in the building of their own village libraries. Given this, it is very important to understand the functions of information and knowledge transfer, and to think critically about the ways that oral practices and new literacy practices may be blended—within the context of these village libraries and beyond.

The literature reveals little about how mothers/grandmothers in rural African villages share important cultural knowledge with their children through oral stories. While there is quite a collection of research about the information needs and information-seeking habits of people in Africa (Ikoja-Odongo and Ocholla, 2004; Camble, 1994; Aboyade, 1987; Durrani, 1985; Kempson, 1986; Mchombu, 1996; Kaniki, 1994), and about women's information needs and information-seeking habits (Fairer-Wessels, 1990; Nginwa, Ocholla, and Ojiambo, 1997), it is difficult to find research based in sub-Saharan Africa about how Ugandan mothers *share* cultural information with their young children through stories, the links of these stories to literacy practices such as reading, and, specifically, the themes represented within these stories. Efforts to improve literacy rates in the developing world are ongoing; at the same time, there is real value in understanding the current modes of cultural information exchange—both context and meaning.

This will allow for the thoughtful support and integration of these practices, not their replacement, as reading cultures are established.

The role of the rural village library

This study in this example is framed by ongoing research on the impact of the rural village library in Africa, which must itself be understood within the context of access to reading materials and the importance of literacy. One of the legacies of colonialism on the African continent is the widespread illiteracy and entrenched poverty that interfere with its people's full participation in the global economy.

A frequently cited reason for the astounding illiteracy rate in Uganda and, indeed, on the entire continent, is the dysfunctional public library system left over from the days of colonialism (Alemna, 1995; Mostert, 1998; Rosenberg, 1993; Stilwell, 1989, 1991). These public libraries, generally located outside rural communities and thus inconvenient to most of the population, are based on a Western model of information transmission oriented toward the culture, needs, and language of the African colonizers, whether they were English, French, German, Italian, or Portuguese. In the public library system, "the needs of the colonized were subservient, if considered at all" (Stilwell, 1989, p. 264) and have historically functioned as "a reflection of colonial interests and priorities" (Ekpe, 1979, p. 5). Consequently, Africans across the continent developed distrust of printed material (and possibly of literacy itself) because of its use in the spread of pro-colonial propaganda (Stilwell, 1989). Stilwell (1989, 1991) has carefully documented colonizers' intentional efforts to block curious Africans from using the public library system altogether.

These public library systems are currently underfunded and dysfunctional because their collections are largely irrelevant to the needs of a continent struggling to become literate. Thus, an alternate model of an African library was created to fill in the void created in the wake of these inadequate Western-style traditional systems. The concept of the rural community library originated in 1968 and seems to have caught on in a variety of African countries, including South Africa (Mostert, 1998; Stilwell, 1989, 1991), Nigeria (Aboyade, 1984), Ghana (Alemna, 1995), Tanzania (Mchombu, 1984), Kenya (Durrani, 1985; Philip, 1980), Botswana, Mali, Zimbabwe (Sturges, 1994), and Burkina Faso (Dent Goodman, 2008; Kevane and Sissao, 2008).

Since 2001, the Kitengesa Community Library has been an example of a rural village library in action. Located in the Masaka District of Uganda, the library offers printed material in the native language of Luganda, adult literacy classes, children's storytelling times, and holdings that reflect the specific needs and interests of the local residents, such as farming, medical health, and child-rearing (Dent, 2006b; Dent and Yannotta, 2005; Parry, in press-a, in press-b). Its pervasive impact has been meticulously documented in a series of qualitative research studies conducted in the critical domains of high school scholastic achievement (Dent, 2006a), literacy acquisition (Dent and Yannotta, 2005), establishment of a reading culture (Parry, in press-a, in press-b), and economic development within the community (Dent, 2007). Quantitative research conducted on rural community libraries in Burkina Faso largely supports these qualitative findings (Kevane and Sissao, 2008).

Residents of Kitengesa are for the most part without running water or mains electricity, although recent efforts have seen the laying of pipe and other implements necessary to pipe water to the village. Villagers make a living by small-scale farming and some fishing. The Kitengesa Community Library was funded primarily by a United Nations One Percent for Development Fund grant, and constructed in 2001 on the grounds of the Kitengesa Comprehensive Secondary School by a professor from Hunter College, her husband (a former resident of the village), and the headmaster of the secondary school. The library was built to serve the needs of the community—mainly students and teachers— as well as provide service to village members. The library currently features a collection of about 2,000 books and the building can comfortably seat 24. There are two librarians and a few student library assistants who work in the library in exchange for school fees. The students of the secondary school are automatically members of the library, and community members pay $1 per year for library use and borrowing privileges. Anyone in the community can use the library facility to sit and read or study at any time—this does not cost anything. Currently, there are about 500 members of the library, and the library is open a total of 77 hours per week. As of summer 2009, the library remained the only public structure in the village with electricity. The lights in the library are powered by solar panels.

The Kitengesa Community Library served as the home base for this project, although not all of the mothers/ grandmothers were members.

Elements of the project's methods

Convenience sampling was used to select the transcripts used in the study. Twelve semi-structured interviews with women from the rural Ugandan village of Kitengesa conducted during the summer of 2009 as part of a larger study were selected. Five of the women were members of the Kitengesa

Community Library, seven were non-members. The mothers/ grandmothers were from roughly similar socioeconomic backgrounds. All were literate, although the literacy levels varied. All had completed some level of either primary or secondary schooling. Participants answered 40 questions as part of a semi-structured interview. Questions focused on the reading habits, library use and literacy practices of the mothers/grandmothers, as well as their socioeconomic and health status. The answers to two specific questions generated the data for this study: Do you ever tell your children stories? and, If yes, can you provide an example of a story that you tell to your children?

Interviews with the Ugandan mothers were conducted over the course of the two-week period. The interviews were conducted in the village library by a team of two researchers and one translator. The interviews took approximately one hour to administer. Transcripts for this study were selected from 51 interviews based on the examples of stories shared in answer to the two questions stated above. Stories with more detail and elaboration were selected above those shorter examples where the storyteller only shared a brief summary of a story, or a few sentences. The interviews were translated simultaneously (from the native Luganda to English) through an interpreter during the actual interview. The videotaped sessions were later transcribed into text by a doctoral student coding team from Long Island University's clinical psychology doctoral program.

The actual coding of the data was done by the primary researcher, and proceeded according to the steps explicated by Auerbach and Silverstein (2003):

- Explicitly state research concerns and theoretical framework.
- Select the relevant text for further analysis.

- Record repeating ideas by grouping together related passages of text
- Organize themes by grouping repeated ideas into coherent categories
- Develop theoretical constructs by grouping themes into more abstract concepts consistent with the theoretical framework
- Create a theoretical narrative by retelling the participant's story in terms of the theoretical constructs. (2003, p. 43)

In addition to the manual analysis of the content, the same text was visualized using the free online visualization software ManyEyes (www.manyeyes.com), which produced visual representations of certain word groupings. The relevant text was also imported into the content analysis software Tinderbox, which allowed for certain properties associated with the mothers' interviews to be represented visually and examined at once using an object-oriented interface.

What the content analysis revealed

This section provides an overview of the initial outcomes for this study, primarily to demonstrate how a study using this particular qualitative approach might evolve. The context for the initial outcomes are also discussed (including a very brief overview of associated literature) in order to highlight how findings from a grounded theory approach might be framed.

The study produced seventeen repeating ideas, seven themes, and finally, two theoretical constructs, based on groupings of themes that emerged from repeating ideas in each of the stories (see Table 8.1). The constructs are:

Table 8.1	Summary of Repeating Ideas, Themes, and Theoretical Constructs

Repeating Ideas
Animal
Garden
Manual work/labor
Marriage
Monster/Beast
God/Faith
Laziness
Death
Walking alone
"Njabala"
Girls as main characters
Twins
School
Disobedience
Food/Water
Husband (man or beast)
Nothing is free/taking things for granted

Themes (categories)

Fear
Role of women in marriage
Failure to fulfill the marriage duties
Physical labor as a means of providing sustenance
Pitfalls of not working hard
Children and obedience
Role of girls/women in society

Theoretical constructs

Fear as a conforming influence on young girls' gender roles
Fear as a conforming influence on childhood obedience

Source: Author.

Research has demonstrated that oral stories are a powerful medium for communication within cultures. Stories can communicate shared values within a group, contribute to social stability, and promote and maintain the social status quo (MacFadyen, 2004). Oral stories in particular play a key role in the transmission of cultural capital, and support the ongoing maintenance of beliefs, morals, and rules (MacFadyen, 2004). Similarly, African stories provide a means to share moral and cultural messages, and a way to "express ambiguous emotions involved in close interpersonal interaction that we all share" within a culturally established framework (Jacobson-Widding, 1992, p. 19). These stories can also "epitomize the structural and structuring principles of the public, social order" (Jacobson-Widding, 1992, p. 10). Psychoanalytic constructs can also be seen within the context of African stories. Self-identity, group identity, individuation, and mother-child attachment are not uncommon themes, often framed by cultural practices such as the "weaning trauma" discussed by Jacobson-Widding during a study of the Manyika people of Zimbabwe (1993, p. 12).

Two specific constructs emerged during this study. The meta-construct was that of fear, which appeared to be used in a number of the stories in a variety of contexts. This major theme was often intertwined with other concepts such as gender roles (for girls), societal norms, and social control. These fear elements, represented by some of the repeating ideas and themes culled from the transcripts, are transmitted verbally through the mothers' stories, as Rachman (1977) illustrates:

> Information-giving is an inherent part of child-rearing and is carried on by parents and peers in an almost unceasing fashion, particularly in the child's earliest years. It is probable that informational and instructional processes provide the basis for most of our commonly encountered fears of everyday life. Fears acquired informationally are more likely to be mild than severe. (1997, p. 384)

In addition to the element of fear in many of the stories, most of the stories featured girls as the main characters, and many times these characters met with some fateful end. A number of the stories focused on marriage, and the importance of fulfilling the "marital duties." Disaster would befall any girl who behaved badly. The traditions and norms associated with marriage differ from culture to culture in Africa, although certain customs associated with marriage in some African cultures—polygyny and child betrothal, for instance—have been characterized as degrading of women (Perlman and Moal, 1963). Physical abuse and unequitable physical labor by the wife both in the home and on the land have been cited as frequent features of marriage in some cultures as well. Conceptualizations about the nature of marriage in the village where this study took place were not a part of this study. However, the content of the stories do suggest an emphasis on the role of the girl/woman in relation to marriage. The story of "Balinda" is a good example of a tale that combines the marriage and gender role element with that of fear:

> At one time when they go to the forest to fetch firewood. So people are fetching firewood, collecting firewood for hut. She was seated, Balinda was seated. So the beastie came, so in the process of bringing that firewood, that beast had to marry Balinda. When Balinda put the firewood on her head, that Beastie followed Balinda. So the beast was like "Balinda, wait for me!" Balinda was crying, then her friends were like "you never wanted to collect the firewood, let it follow you . . . let the beast follow you." So they come with it home, Balinda come with this beast at home. So the beast told the parents that "we made an agreement with the Balinda, that I have to collect her firewood, and every time I have to take her home and she has to cook for me." So, Balinda cried. So what we learn in this story, that you have to work in this world, not sit. If you want free things, you

end up getting what? Problems. So Balinda was married to the . . . To the monster, to the beast. The beast, yes, because she was lazy.

In the story, "Balinda" must marry a beast because she failed to do her chores and collect firewood. It illustrates that terrible things happen to lazy girls. This was a repeated idea in a number of stories, including the story of "Njabala"—a young girl who was married but lost her husband because she "failed to fulfill all the marital duties." "Njabala" was told by a number of the mothers and grandmothers. As well, the story of "Whengivla" featured a young girl, married, whose husband also left her because "she was very lazy at home."

Muris et al. (2010) found that children's "fear beliefs" could be influenced by a parent sharing negative information with the child (p. 341). This study did not assess the reactions of children as they listened to these stories, so it is impossible to know for certain the impact that the stories had, but a number of the stories told by the mothers and grandmothers feature elements that might provoke fear in the listener. Consider the suicide story:

> That once upon a time, there was a man who married his wife. They produced kid, two kids. That there came a dry spell, famine. The mommy goes to look for the kid, goes to look for the food. She comes back and then finds the dad has committed suicide. The mommy comes back finds the children were just alone. The dad has committed suicide. People gathered when mommy came back, she was so alone and people gathered. That the dead body was beaten . . . The dead body. Was beaten and buried. But after bury, burial and funeral, that after the family just dismantled like the

mom went in a different direction and the kids went away because the mom could not look after these. The story ends there. This one to bring the kinds from the same thing the dad did. So when they see the dead body being beaten they can't also commit suicide because they will also fear to be beaten. After they're dead.

The story is meant to instill enough fear in the listener so as to discourage them from ever committing suicide. The image of a dead body being beaten is certainly enough to instill this level of fear, especially if that image is of a parent.

One obvious message is that children who disobey a parent are likely to wind up hurt, or in some kind of trouble. Fear is embodied in many of the stories by monsters and beasts. In one story, a child is walking alone at night, against advice, and a creature attaches to the child's back:

> There was a child that used to walk at night, many times. And there was a mask-like creature that attached to her, to her back when she was . . . Walking at night. And that one teaches children not to move at night.

In another example of a story, one twin is eaten by a monster because they disobey a parent:

> These two twins went to the garden. And mom told them that you know what, it's time to go back home. So one decided to remain in the garden then the one come with the mom. The one who remained behind was eaten by a beast.

The storytellers in this study reported that their stories were rarely told for entertainment—they were always told with a purpose in mind. As one mother stated when asked about her story, "It teaches children to behave." Jacobson-Widding (1993) supports this notion, and suggests that teaching her children obedience, correct behavior and good manners are "a woman's prime duty" in some African cultures. "Unconditional obedience to those who are bigger than yourself" is a key message (1993, p. 10). There is thus an emphasis on the transfer of knowledge associated with this concept.

These stories should also be understood within the context of present-day life in Uganda. During the researchers' stay in the village, a number of adults and children talked about the dangers of child kidnappings and child sacrifice by "witch-doctors." It was a subject frequently on the minds of the villagers, despite the fact that the majority of these acts are rumored to take place in the northern part of the country. This could certainly be understood as a reason for keeping young children from wandering the roads alone at night.

This project is just one example of the types of research that may be facilitated in a qualitative manner. Such approaches allow for intense examination of phenomenon, and for these explorations to take place *in vivo* (within a natural setting). In this case, future research would be based solely on the further examination of the two theoretical constructs, which would be transformed into research questions and related hypotheses. For instance, a research question related to the first construct, fear as a conforming influence on young girls' gender roles, might be: Do elements of fear in told oral stories play a role in shaping Ugandan girls' behavior in early childhood? A research question related to the second construct, fear as a conforming influence on childhood obedience, might be: Do elements of fear in told oral stories play a role in shaping Ugandan children's obedience? Related hypotheses and means of testing them would need to be formed. These are only two examples of possible research questions. The data are incredibly rich, and there are a number of other possibilities that might also be worth pursuing.

This is certainly not the typical library research project—but it is an example of the many ways that the study of libraries and related phenomena in all forms may be accomplished.

References

Aboyade, B.O. (1984) Communications potentials of the library for non-literates: An experiment in providing information services in a rural setting. *Libri International Journal of Libraries and Information Services*, 34(3): 243–62.

Aboyade, B.O. (1987) *The Provision of Information for Rural Development*. Ibadan, Nigeria: Fountain Publishers.

Alemna, A. (1995) Community libraries: An alternative to public libraries in Africa. *Library Review*, 44(7): 40–4.

Auerbach, C. and Silverstein, L. (2003) *Qualitative Data: An Introduction to Coding and Analysis?*. New York: New York University Press.

Camble, E. (1994) The information environment of rural development workers in Borno state, Nigeria. *African Journal of Library, Archives and Information Science*, 4: 99–106.

Dent, V. (2006a) Observations of school library impact at two rural Ugandan schools. *New Library World*, 107(9/10): 403–21.

Dent, V. (2006b) Modelling the rural community library: Characteristics of the Kitengesa Library in rural Uganda. *New Library World*, 107(1/2): 16–30.

Dent, V.F. (2007) Local economic development in Uganda and the connection to rural community libraries and literacy. *New Library World*, 108(5/6): 203–17.

Dent, V. and Yannotta, L. (2005) A rural community library in Uganda: A study of its use and users. *Libri International Journal of Libraries and Information Services*, 55(1): 39–55.

Dent Goodman, V. (2008) Rural library services: Historical development and modern-day examples from West Africa. *New Library World*, 109(11/12): 512–32.

Durrani, S. (1985) Rural information in Kenya. *Information Development*, 1: 149–57.

Ekpe, F.C. (1979) The colonial situation and library development in Nigeria. *International Library Review*, 11: 5–18.

Fairer-Wessels, F.A. (1990) Basic community information needs of urban black women in Mamelodi, Pretoria, South Africa. *South African Journal of Library and Information Science*, 58: 359–69.

Ikoja-Odongo, R. and Ocholla, D. (2004) Information-seeking behavior of the informal sector entrepreneurs: The Uganda experience. *Libri International Journal of Libraries and Information Services*, 54: 54–66.

Jacobson-Widding, A. (1992) Pits, pots and snakes. An anthropological approach to ancient African symbols. *Nordic Journal of African Studies*, 1(1): 5–27.

Jacobson-Widding, A. (1993) Individual identity in African story telling. *Nordic Journal of African Studies*, 2(1): 5–31.

Kaniki, A.M. (1994) Information seeking and information providers among Zambian farmers. *Libri International Journal of Libraries and Information Services*, 41: 147–69.

Kempson, E. (1986) Information for self-reliance and self-determination: The role of community information services. *IFLA Journal*, 12(3): 182–91.

Kevane, M. and Sissao, A. (2008) How much do village libraries increase reading? Results from a survey of 10th graders in Burkina Faso. *Libri International Journal of Libraries and Information Services*, 58(3): 202–10.

Macfadyen, L. (2004) From the spoken to the written: The changing cultural role of folk and fairy tales. *Journal of Graduate Liberal Studies*, 143–53. Retrieved from *https://circle.ubc.ca/bitstream/handle/2429/1328/MacfadyenJGLS.pdf?sequence=1*.

Mchombu, K.J. (1984) Development of library and documentation services in Tanzania: Problems of strategy and tactics. *Information Processing and Management*, 20(4): 559–69.

Mchombu, K.J. (1996) A survey of information needs for rural development. *Resource Sharing and Information Networks*, 12(1): 75–81.

Mostert, B.J. (1998) Community libraries: The concept and its application—with particular reference to a South African library system. *International Information and Library Review*, 30: 71–85.

Muris, P., van Zwol, L., Huijding, J. and Mayer, B. (2010) Mom told me scary things about this animal: Parents installing fear beliefs in their children via the verbal information pathway. *Behaviour Research and Therapy*, 48: 341–6.

Nginwa, P., Ocholla, D.N. and Ojiambo, J.B. (1997) Media accessibility and utilization by Kenyan rural women. *International Information and Library Review*, 29: 45–66.

Ong, W. (2002) *Orality and Literacy: The Technologizing of the Word*, 2nd edition. New York: Routledge.

Parry, K. (2004) Opportunities for girls: A community library project in Uganda. In B. Norton and A. Pavlenko (eds.), *Gender and English language learners* (pp. 81–94). Alexandria, VA: TESOL.

Parry, K. (in press-a) A library for learning: Experiences of students in Uganda.

Parry, K. (in press-b) Books for African readers: Borrowing patterns at Kitengesa Community Library, Masaka, Uganda.

Perlman, I.M. and Moal, M.P. (eds.) (1963) *Women of Tropical Africa*. Berkeley: University of California Press/ H.M. Wright.

Philip, A. (1980) Organization and management of rural (village) libraries. *Maktaba*, 7(2): 45–50.

Rachman, S. (1977) The conditioning theory of fear acquisition: A critical examination. *Behaviour Research and Therapy*, 15(5): 375–87.

Rosenberg, D. (1993) Rural community resource centres: A sustainable option for Africa? *Information Development*, 9(1/2): 29–35.

Stilwell, C. (1989) Community libraries: A brief review of their origins and nature with particular reference to South Africa. *Journal of Librarianship*, 21(4): 260–9.

Stilwell, C. (1991) Community libraries: A viable alternative to the public library in South Africa? *Progressive Librarian*, 4 (Winter): 17–27.

Sturges, P. (1994) Using grey literature in informal information services in Africa. *Journal of Documentation*, 50: 273–90.

9

Learning more about qualitative research

Abstract: This chapter provides some suggestions for ways in which librarians might educate themselves about the history, theories, and practice of qualitative work. A list of professional organizations and resources is provided.

Key words: professional organizations, libraries, research workshops, qualitative research conferences.

Most of us who are librarians by profession have never formally learned research methods and practice. It is not uncommon to encounter librarians who are learning about research methods for the first time, on the job, when faced with the need to do so in order to study some relevant phenomenon.

The need for librarians to be familiar with research methods may not be seen as critical by some, but understanding how to conduct applied research is a skill that can be of great benefit to librarians and others in information settings. This is not to suggest that librarians need to become researchers—in most cases, that is not a part of the job description nor is it necessary. However, when developments in technology and the digital landscape require a closer look, these skills may come in handy.

There are resources for librarians who want to learn more about research practices. Professional organizations are a good place to start. Sensing the need for heightened discussion about the role of research in the modern library, organizations such as the Library Research Roundtable (LRRT) of the American Library Association have recently focused on the topic, with such presentations as "Research from the field: Increasing the competitive edge and impact of libraries' people, services, and technologies" and "Research to understand users: Issues and approaches" being presented at the 2010 American Library Association Annual Conference (ALA, 2010). LRRT also provides research seminars to help practitioners integrate research practices into everyday library activities, such as the "Integrating practice and research" seminar held in October 2010.

One way for librarians to learn about research is by working with other researchers. Interest in improving these types of collaborations is evidenced by grant opportunities, such as the 2008 research grant funded by the Special Libraries Association (SLA). The project investigated emerging roles for librarians outside of the library: "Several non-traditional roles for information professionals have been established in the sciences to support biomedical research. However, there is little precedent for information professionals to participate in biomedical research collaboration beyond the role of a librarian as an information researcher" (SLA, 2008).

The Association for Information Systems, maintained by noted information systems researcher Michael Myers (2009), has a helpful website which features a section entitled "Qualitative Research in Information Systems." Librarians might also be interested in the Association for Qualitative Research website (*http://www.aqr.org.uk/*) (2010), and the Reference and User Services Association's (RUSA, 2010) "Doing Qualitative Research" website, which also has a number of informative resources. The

Intute research clearinghouse website (*http://www.intute .ac.uk/cgi-bin/browse.pl?id=120997*), which is co-sponsored by the Joint Information Systems Committee (JISC), also features a wide range of qualitative resources (Intute, 2010). There are also resources for specific qualitative approaches, such as Barney Glaser's Grounded Theory Institute website (Dr Glaser is one of the original founders of grounded theory) (2010) (*http://www.groundedtheory.org/*). Finally, "The Qualitative Report" (*http://www.nova.edu/ssss/QR/ tqrnews2010.html*) is a website that provides links to many qualitative resources including conferences, publications, reviews, and the latest research (2010).

Collaboration is perhaps one of the most effective ways for librarians to learn more about and become engaged in research practices, regardless of the methodology. In academic settings, librarians might work with faculty in various departments that have similar interests. The ethnography studies at the University of Rochester and Rutgers University (see Chapter 6) are great examples. In both cases, anthropologists from outside the library were brought in to work with librarians and library staff, to guide the ethnographic process and, most importantly, to teach others as much as possible about ethnographic work. The sharing of knowledge in both cases was just as important as the research projects—the skills learned by the librarians were valuable and applicable beyond the study itself.

Librarians do have a history of partnering with faculty for information literacy and instructional projects (Isbell and Broaddus, 1993; Bruce, 2001; Black et al., 2001; Jackson, 2007), but librarians as research partners in the disciplines are less common. Research issues within library and information settings are obviously different from those in the various disciplines, such as biology and chemistry. However, disciplines such as psychology, information science, communication science, and computer science are areas where there may be shared research questions. Library and Information Studies programs are also a natural alliance. Distinguishing theoretical exploration from research with a practical application is critical—while current research on natural language searching might be highly relevant for librarians (Lee, 2010), research on root finding algorithms (Al-Shawakfa et al., 2010) might not be. Usability issues may be of interest to librarians and to faculty studying human computer interaction; cognitive aspects of information search and retrieval practices may be of interest to psychologists and librarians. Library settings that serve a broader public, such as public libraries, educational institutions, museums, and public service departments may be organizations interested in practical research projects that are focused on community outreach and civic engagement.

In addition to these opportunities for collaboration, Pickton (2007) suggests that there are benefits to the individual, the organization, and to the profession for librarians who conduct research. Veldof (1999) supports this idea, suggesting that research is no longer a luxury: "Creating and analyzing Pareto and control charts, customer satisfaction surveys, needs assessment focus group interviews, and other data methods have since become an integral part of everyday work at the Library" (p. 31).

For those librarians who are interested in learning about research methods as both a practical and an educational endeavor, taking classes at a local college or university might be an option. Research methods courses at the undergraduate or graduate levels typically focus on both quantitative and qualitative approaches, and can be a good way to get started. Classes can also provide an environment to develop and test possible research questions and obtain feedback from instructors. These classes might be offered within Sociology, Psychology, Education, Library and Information Studies, and Information Science departments. Anthropology departments might offer courses on ethnomethodology and ethnographic research. There are also various conferences, workshops, and institutes that might be worth investigating. The International Institute of Qualitative Inquiry (*http:// www.iiqi.org/*); the Current and Emerging Trends in Qualitative Research Workshop (*http://www.esomar.org/ index.php/workshops-trends-in-qualitative-research.html*); and the Ethnographic and Qualitative Research Conference (*http://www.cedarville.edu/event/eqrc/*) are just a few. There are also library-specific events that librarians can take advantage of. The Association of Research Libraries (ARL) sponsors the Service Quality Evaluation Academy, a five-day workshop which aims to "enhance the pool of librarians with advanced assessment skills by teaching quantitative and qualitative methods for assessing and improving outcomes and service quality" (ARL, 2010). The Qualitative and Quantitative Methods in Libraries International Conference (*http://www.isast.org/qqml2010 .html*) is growing in popularity, and the corresponding publication *Qualitative and Quantitative Methods in Libraries Theory and Applications* (Katsirikou and Skiadas, 2009) might also be helpful.

There are many ways for librarians and others to learn more about qualitative research. It can be a time-consuming and intense endeavor, but certainly worth the effort. Librarians fortunate enough to learn more about these methods should make it a point to share their new skills and knowledge with others in their organization, making it more likely that qualitative methods might be considered as a way to investigate research questions and improve user services.

References

Al-Shawakfa, E., Al-Badarneh, A., Shatnawi, S., Al-Rabab'ah, K. and Bani-Ismail, B. (2010) A comparison study of some Arabic root finding algorithms. *Journal of the American Society for Information Science and Technology*, 61(5): 1015–24.

American Library Association Annual Conference (ALA) (2010) Retrieved from *http://www.ala.org/ala/mgrps/rts/lrrt/index.cfm*.

Association for Qualitative Research (2010) Retrieved from *http://www.aqr.org.uk/*.

Association of Research Libraries (ARL) (2010) Retrieved from *http://www.arl.org/stats/statsevents/sqacademy/index.shtml*.

Black, C., Crest, S. and Volland, M. (2001) Building a successful information literacy infrastructure on the foundation of librarian–faculty collaboration. *Research Strategies*, 18(3): 215–25.

Bruce, C. (2001) Faculty-librarian partnerships in Australian higher education: Critical dimensions. *Reference Services Review*, 29(2): 106–16.

Grounded Theory Institute (2010) Retrieved from *http://www.groundedtheory.com/*.

Intute Research Clearinghouse (2010) Retrieved from *http://www.intute.ac.uk/*.

Isbell, D. and Broaddus, D. (1993) Teaching writing and research as inseparable: A faculty-librarian teaching team. *Reference Services Review*, 23(4): 51–62.

Jackson, P. (2007) Integrating information literacy into blackboard: Building campus partnerships for successful student learning. *Journal of Academic Librarianship*, 33(4): 454–61.

Katsirikou, A. and Skiadas, C. (2009) Qualitative and quantitative methods in libraries. Theory and applications. *Proceedings of the International Conference on QQML 2009*. Hackensack, NJ: World Scientific.

Lee, J.H. (2010) Analysis of user needs and information features in natural language queries seeking music information. *Journal of the American Society for Information Science and Technology*, 61(5): 1025–45.

Myers, M. (2009) Qualitative research in information systems website. Retrieved from *http://www.qual .auckland.ac.nz/*.

Pickton, M. (2007) Breakout session one: Notes from the library and information research group speakers. *Library and Information Research*, 31(97): 2.

The Qualitative Report (2010) Retrieved from *http://www .nova.edu/ssss/QR/index.html*.

Reference and User Services Association (RUSA) (2010) Retrieved from *http://alapress.org/ala/mgrps/divs/rusa/ sections/rss/rsssection/rsscomm/rssresstat/qualitresrch.cfm#*.

Special Libraries Association (SLA) (2008) Retrieved from *http://collaborativelibrarians.org/sla-research-grant/*.

Veldof, J. (1999) Data driven decisions: Using data to inform process changes in libraries. *Library and Information Science Research*, 21(1): 31–46.

10

Qualitative research as a way to explore change in the modern world

Abstract: This chapter summarizes the book and reinforces the applicability of qualitative research within the library and information services environments.

Change is a part of our lives in many ways. We as humans and the world we live in continue to evolve in ways that we are mostly unaware of. There are also the obvious changes— some trivial, some more substantial—that give us pause. A number of years ago, the American insurance company GEICO had a series of television commercials that featured a couple of cavemen who found themselves in some uncomfortable situations as they tried to navigate our modern world. Those commercials were popular, and very funny. Five years on, GEICO has a new set of television commercials, featuring a range of characters, including a pig named Maxwell, who, strapped into a child's car seat in an SUV, cries "Wee wee wee" all the way home. Again, very funny. It is not unrealistic to assume that, within the next few years, GEICO will reveal another set of television commercials, simply because after a while the public tires of even the funniest offerings. Libraries and information settings do not have the luxury of changing user experience strategies, changing services and changing resources every few years in order to keep a demanding public satisfied. What librarians and others do have is the ability to try and figure out what users are doing, when, where, and why. Qualitative research can provide a framework for these endeavors. The most beneficial takeaway from this book is that taking the time to learn more about qualitative research, how it has been used in other settings and how it can benefit those of us who work in library and information settings, is important. It makes sense, and it is useful. It can also be a radical approach, a postmodern way of looking at user need, assessment, and evaluation. It is a way to learn more about ourselves and how we operate in our work environments.

Finally, there seems to be a certain synergy between the use of qualitative approaches within library environments and realizing the elusive user experience that we hear about so often. Libraries are story- and data-rich. If we listen, and watch, we can learn far more about our users than statistics alone can reveal. Along the way, it is possible that we can also learn about ourselves, and more about the human elements that define our profession.

Index

A.C. Nielsen Company, 2, 35–8
academic library, 85–90
   Association of College and
     Research Libraries, 87–8
   future assumptions, 88
   trends, 87
*African Systems of Kinship and
   Marriage*, 49
Amazon, 92
*Argonauts of the Western
   Pacific*, 49
Association for Information
   Systems, 178
Association for Qualitative
   Research, 178
Association of College and
   Research Libraries
   (ACRL), 76
   academic libraries future
     assumptions, 88
   trends impacting academic
     library, 87
Association of Research Libraries
   (ARL), 90–1, 95

"Balinda," 168–9
Barney Glaser's Grounded
   Theory Institute website,
   179
Bernays, E., 110

Blackboard, 138
*Broadband Adoption and Use in
   America*, 83

case study, 15–16
Centre for Information Behaviour
   and the Evaluation of
   Research (CIBER), 76
cloud computing, 90–3
Coalition for Networked
   Information (CNI), 76
collaboration, 179
*Coming of Age in New Jersey:
   College and American
   Culture*, 34
Coming of Age in Samoa, 49
community analysis, 50–1
Community Analysis Research
   Institute (CARI) model, 51
Computer Anxiety Index, 128
Connaway, L.S., 81, 85
constant comparative method,
   127
consumerism, 110–11
content analysis, 22–4
convenience sampling, 163–4
Council on Library and
   Information Resources
   (CLIR), 86
Csikszentmihalyi, M., 117

Current and Emerging Trends in
   Qualitative Research
   Workshop, 181
"cyberkids," 79

data analysis, 22–4
data coding, 164–5
design by neglect *see* unintentional
   design
"design thinking," 113–14
"Designing Better Libraries" *blog*,
   112
digital immigrants, 80
digital literacy, 82
digital natives, 79, 80–1
disruptive technologies, 134–9
Dynamic Information/Frequent
   Activities, 138
Dynamic Information/Infrequent
   Activities, 138

Ethnographic and Qualitative
   Research Conference,
   181
ethnographic research
   historical application, 50–6
   implications and challenges,
      66–8
   key concepts, 45–9
   paradigms, 47
   practices in library settings,
      45–68
   quantitative and qualitative
      approaches to library
      research, 64–6
   recent examples in library
      environments, 56–64
   anthropologist in the library,
      57–8

California State University
   Fresno Henry Madden
   Library ethnographic
   study, 58
information systems design
   and evaluation, 60–4
MIT student photo diary
   study, 58
pre-schoolers' use of public
   libraries, 57
Rutgers University Libraries
   student behaviors and
   website redesign study,
   59–60
Uganda rural village library
   study, 60
University of Rochester
   Libraries study of
   undergraduates, 58–9
ethnography, 46
ethnomethodology, 66
"experience economy," 109

flow, 117–20
   associated progressive states of
      mind and skills, 118
focus groups, 13–14
framing, 115
Freud, S., 109–10

Gartner Group, 135
Geertz, C., 47
Godin, S., 112–13
Google, 92
Google App Engine, 92
Google Mobile, 95
Google SMS, 95
Gribbons, W., 108
grounded theory, 20–2, 126, 165

HyperResearch, 133

information capture, 139
information-giving, 167
information literacy, 82
information seeking, 78
International Federation of Library
    Associations and
    Institutions (IFLA), 96
International Institute of
    Qualitative Inquiry, 181
interviews, 14–15
Intute research clearinghouse
    website, 178–9

Joopz, 95
*Juggling Food and Feelings:
    Emotional Balance in the
    Workplace*, 149

Kitengesa Community Library,
    162–3

LibQual, 64
libraries, 2–4
library
    explore as workplace, 147–51
    qualitative approaches, 185–6
library and information science,
    66–8
Library and Information Studies
    (LIS), 180
library anxiety, 125–30
    definition, 126
Library Anxiety Scale, 127, 128
Library Journal, 112
Library Quarterly, 67
library research
    current trends, 78

generational differences and
    digital landscape, 79–85
matrix, 96–8
    use the Brainstorming
    Phase, 97
role of technology through
    research, 90–5
cloud computing, 90–3, 91–3
mobile technology, 94–5
state of research and academic
    library, 85–90
trends, professional literature
    and users to create canvas,
    75–98
Library Research Roundtable, 178
library settings
    ethnographic research practices,
    45–68
    historical application, 50–6
    implications and challenges,
    66–8
    key concepts, 45–9
    quantitative and qualitative
    approaches to library
    research, 64–6
    recent examples in library
    environments, 56–64
library website, 130–4

ManyEyes, 165
medicine, 40–1
"millennials," 79, 81–2, 85
Mobifeeds, 95
mobile technology, 94–5
Moodle, 150
Morville, P., 109
*My Freshman Year: What a
    Professor Learned by
    Becoming a Student*, 34

narrative analysis, 159
narratives, 16–19
naturalistic inquiry, 55
Naven: A Survey of the Problems Suggested by a Composite Picture of the Culture of a New Guinea Tribe Drawn from Three Points of View, 49
"net generation," 79
Nielsen, J., 115
"Nintendo Generation," 79
"Njabala," 169
No Brief Candle: Reconceiving Research Libraries for the 21st Century, 86
North Carolina State University Libraries Mobile (2010a), 131
nursing, 38–40

Online Computer Library Centre (OCLC), 76
oral stories, 166–7
orality, 159

participant observation, 11–13
People Meters, 36
PEW Internet & American Life Project, 91, 94–5
place-aware technology, 138
professional organisations, 177–8
psychoanalytic constructs, 167
psychology, 40–1
public library system, 161–2

Qualitative and Quantitative Methods in Libraries International Conference, 181
qualitative content analysis, 165–72
repeating ideas, themes and theoretical constructs, 166
qualitative research, 4–5, 7–26, 131, 177–81
changes in the modern world, 185–6
data analysis, 22–4
data gathering, 10–20
case studies, 15–16
focus groups, 13–14
interviews, 14–15
participant observation, 11–13
stories and narratives, 16–19
unobtrusive methods, 19–20
description, 8–10
exploring the library as workplace, 147–51
grounded theory, 20–2
non-library setting, 33–41
A.C. Nielsen Company, 35–8
academic environment, 33–4
medicine and mental health, 40–1
nursing, 38–40
qualitative data, 24–6
service-related challenges of librarians, 125–39
disruption and information seeker, 134–9
library anxiety, 125–30
library website, 130–4

study of global libraries,
157–72
content analysis, 165–72
project methods, 163–5
rationale, 158–61
rural village library, 161–3
understanding user experience
in library settings,
107–20
design, broken-ness, and
library user experience,
111–15
flow as an element, 117–20
self and user experience,
109–11
Useit.com on UX research,
115–17
Queensborough Public Library,
77–8

Reference and User Services
Association, 178
Report on the Information Needs
of Communities in a
Democracy (2009), 83
research, 1–5
"research agenda," 75–6
rich media research, 34–8
rural village library, 161–3
Rutgers Libraries website,
130–4

Sakai, 138, 150
Scenario Planning for Libraries,
89
scenarios, 89
"screenagers," 79
Self Perception Profile for College
Students (SPPCS), 128

semi-structured interviews,
163–4
Service Quality Evaluation
Academy, 181
set meters, 36
Skweezer, 95
SMS-Web texting services, 95
Social Interdependence Scale (SIS),
128
social networking, 2
Special Libraries Association,
178
Stable Information/Frequent
Activity, 137
Stable Information/Infrequent
Activity, 137
Stingly, G., 51–4
storytelling, 16–19
Study Habits Inventory, 128
Studying Students: The
Undergraduate Research
Project at the University of
Rochester, 50, 59
Stumbleupon, 95
surveys, 10

The Discovery of Grounded
Theory, 20
The Dynamics of Clanship Among
the Tallensi, 49
The Nuer, 49
"The Qualitative Report," 179
The Rutgers Study, 130–4
"The User Experience," 112
theory-generating approach, 127
"thick description" approach, 47
Tinderbox, 165
"transliteracy," 82
Tucson Garbage Study, 20

Uganda, 161–3
unintentional design, 112
Useit.com, 115–17
user experience, 108–9
    design, broken-ness, and
        library user experience,
        111–15
    flow as an element, 117–20
    qualitative approaches to
        understand user experience
        in library settings, 107–20
    self and, 109–11

Useit.com on UX research,
    115–17

video diaries, 150

"Whengivla," 169
workplace ethnographies, 148,
    149
workplace technology, 148

Zinadoo, 95
Zoho, 92

CPSIA information can be obtained at www.ICGtesting.com
264483BV00004B/29/P